The Reluctant Human's Field Guide to

PowerPoint®

Discover the joys and challenges of PowerPoint
and learn to bend it to your will.

Written & illustrated by Stephy Hogan

A Reluctant Human's Guide to PowerPoint® © 2024 by Stephanie Hogan. All rights reserved. No part of this book may be reproduced in any form whatsoever, by photography or xerography or by any other means, by broadcast or transmission, by translation into any kind of language, nor by recording electronically or otherwise, without permission in writing from the author, except by a reviewer, who may quote brief passages in critical articles of reviews.

ISBN: 9798340278197

Library of Congress Control Number: 2024910720

Printed in the United States of America

First Printing: 2024

"Thank you!!!"

Dedicated to my friend Linda who was an absolute ray of sunshine. I didn't get to see her enough.

And thank you to my amazeballs family for tolerating my hyperfixation(s).

Chibi art by @Pistachii

In memory of my cousin Brendan Orr, an amazing human being with mad chef skillz. Miss you 'cuz.

Table of Contents

Introduction 7
Preface 9
Do I HAVE to use PowerPoint? 11
    Let's Speak the Same Language . 20
    The Mac vs. PC Problem 22
    Be an Insider 24
Learn to Get Around 26
    Slide Views 28
    Master Slide and Layouts 29
    Ribbons = Toolbars 30
Interface Showdown 33
    Slide Size 34
    Slide Setup 34
    Guides & Grids 35
    Align & Distribute 36
    Rotate & Flip 36
    Layout Helpers 37
Typography 38
    Font Settings 39
    Alignment 39
    Text Wrap 39
    Bullets & Numbering 40
    Columns 40
    Find Fonts 41
    Glyphs 41
    Leading & Indents 42
    Kerning & Tracking 42
    Text Case 43
    Text Direction 43
    Tabs 43

Color 44
    Swatches 45
    Anatomy of the Color Picker 46
    Chart Colors 47
    Highlighter Color 47
    Slide Fill 48
    Table Colors 48
    Theme Colors 49
Vector Stuff 50
    Pen Tool 51
    Clipping Masks 51
    Shapes 52
    Pathfinder 53
    Icons 54
    Lines & Strokes 54
    Text to Outline 55
Cropping 56
    Content Placeholders 56
    Picture Placeholders 56
    Cropping Photos 57
    Cropping Video 57
    Crop to Shape 57
    Crop to Aspect Ratio 57
Photo Editing 58
    Color Correction 59
    Color Menu 59
    Corrections 59
    Filters 60
    Styles 61
    Removing Backgrounds 62
    Transparency 62
    3D 63

- Tables 64
  - Insert Table 65
  - Table Styles 65
  - Table Elements 66
  - Border Formatting 66
  - Cell Formatting 67
- Charts 68
  - Types of Charts 69
  - Adding Chart Elements 70
  - Quick Layouts & Colors 71
  - Axes 71
  - Series & Data Points 72
  - Data Tables 72
  - Data Labels 73
  - Numbers 73
- Video (and audio) 74
  - Inserting Video & Audio 75
  - Video Format 76
  - Video Playback 77
- Animation 78
- Transitions 82
- Accessibility 87
  - The Accessibility Checker 88
  - Some A11y Design Basics 90
  - Color 90
  - Text 90
  - Alt Text 92
  - Examples of Good Alt Text 92
  - Screen Readers & Reading Order 93
  - The S.C.H.I.T. List 94
    - Sight-related 95
    - Cognition-related 96
    - Hearing-related 97
    - Interaction-related 98
    - Technology-related 99
    - Technology 99
  - Before You Build 100
  - While You Build 101
  - Color & Meaning 102
  - Rainbow for the Colorblind 104
  - Accessibility Checker Gotchas 106
    - Checking Color Contrast 106
    - Alt Text 108
    - Marking Things as Decorative 108
    - Reading Order 109
- Quick Access Toolbar 112
- Keyboard Shortcuts 114
- Skip Links 118
- Paragraph Rules 120
- 3-in-1 Deck 122
- Make Screenshots Look GOOD 124
- Presenting Inclusively 130
- About the author 136

Scan for companion digital content.

There are so many people to thank. First, thanks to my husband for putting up with me on my computer while I was trying to get this book done.

Thank you to my mentors and friends who have taught me, mentored me, laughed with me, and been with me through my who presentation design career and some wonky life changes:

Echo Swinford, Julie Terberg, Glenna Shaw, Charles Cranford, Tony Ramos, Rick Altman, Ric Bretschneider, Nolan Haims, Mike & Jen Parkinson, Sally Z, Tom Howell (who put this book idea in my head). I'm not exhagerating when I say that my life has changed because of all of you.

Now...time to go put that brass pole back up.

Introduction

As a new designer, I *dreaded* Microsoft® PowerPoint™.

It felt clunky—too simple, yet somehow confusing—and it didn't have the graphic features found in my favorite software packages. But since PowerPoint was everywhere and easy for Microsoft users to learn, it became the go-to design tool at most organizations. More and more my clients asked me to use PowerPoint.

I was an Adobe® person stranded in a Microsoft world.

PowerPoint, by design, doesn't have the finesse we expect from dedicated design software. However, I found ways to make it work—or risk losing clients. I soon realized I could design professional graphics, icons, marketing documents, learning materials, posters, flyers, slides, animations, and presentations—all within PowerPoint.

Let me be clear: PowerPoint is *not* a graphics tool. It's a *presentation* tool. And just like any tool, your skills as the user (yep, that's you!) are what make the difference in the final product. After years of trial and error, I discovered that PowerPoint is way more powerful than I ever gave it credit for.

A Reluctant Human's Field Guide to PowerPoint is the easiest, most approachable roadmap I've found for bridging the gap between the Adobe Creative Suite® and PowerPoint. Expect plenty of "a-ha" moments as Stephy Hogan walks you through the parallels between these two worlds in a fun, conversational way. She makes it clear, simple, and best of all, stress-free for designers who use Adobe and want to try designing with PowerPoint.

As you grow your skills, you'll discover surprising perks to using PowerPoint. First, no more endless revisions! Share your file and let the client tweak content as needed. Sure, you might still get the occasional "can you fix this?" request, but it beats making a hundred edits in two days. Second, being a skilled PowerPoint designer is rare, and that makes you stand out. Most designers would rather sketch with flaming pencils than work in PowerPoint. Your willingness to master this tool will set you apart. Third, you'll start working smarter. You'll find creative, clever ways to do more in PowerPoint than you thought possible, without juggling a dozen Adobe tools. I still use the Creative Suite, but now I know when and how to seamlessly integrate PowerPoint to exceed client expectations.

As a graphic designer, be thrilled this book exists! It's about to save you time, money, and—most importantly—your sanity.

—Mike Parkinson, Owner of Billion Dollar Graphics and all-round nice guy

Preface

I love PowerPoint. I really, truly do. But before that happened, I hated PowerPoint. I was not happy to come back from maternity leave only to discover that I was made the lead designer of the PowerPoint team.

I also came back from maternity leave to discover someone had stolen my desk chair—it was one of the last Hermann Millers in the office. I was doubly unhappy.

Being asked to work in PowerPoint hits everyone differently. If you've always considered yourself a designer, whether digital or print, you probably look down on PowerPoint.

If you're a designer who started in another career and has struggled to get to the point where everyone thinks of you as a designer first instead of a defunct chemist... when you're reorged into presentation design, it's a blow to the ego.

But hey, I'm a "if life gives you lemons, make lemon creme brulee" kinda gal. It seems that I have a weird personality quirk where I work inside of some of the most disliked software while absolutely loving it.

Does PowerPoint have issues? What software doesn't. The fun is in forcing PowerPoint to do things it wasn't designed to do in the first place. Replace AfterEffects? Sure! Design printed documents that look like they were made in InDesign? Hell yeah! Create social media assets? Interactive games? Practical jokes for your coworkers? Yes, yes, and YES!

I LOVE bending software to my will. I have control issues.

I'm writing this book so that you can discover all the fun weird shit sooner rather than later. It took me more than a decade to accumulate this knowledge. I want YOU to hit the ground running.

And yes. I did eventually get my chair back.

Do I HAVE to use PowerPoint?

You've either acquired this guide for yourself or some genius of a human being gifted it to you. So, yes. You'll be (or already are) designing in PowerPoint.

Your client wants a thing made in PowerPoint so they can edit it later on their own. You probably just cringed.

You're probably grumpy about it. Been there.

You, like many others, see PowerPoint as the reason why most work meetings are horribly boring and feel like they last an eternity. As the person destined to become The Presentation Designer, you might feel a little indignant.

Been there, too.

Just remember it's not the tool. It's the tool behind the tool. You can make some pretty amazing things with PowerPoint.

Seriously.

You hear "PowerPoint" and this is what you think...

Ten pounds of shit in a 5-pound bag. I actually won an award for that once. No joke. But it wasn't for a presentation. (It was for a 1-inch newspaper ad.)

There are *infinity* examples out there of really horrible slides. You see them every day.

I'm sorry you've had to go through that.

People who don't have any kind of design sense make these. And surprisingly, there are good designers (yes, real ones!) who make shitty slides, too. It's like they open PowerPoint and forget all of their design knowledge. Thankfully, you have me. I won't let that happen to you.

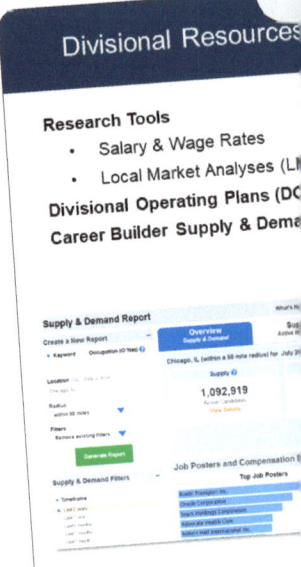

How many of THESE were made in PowerPoint?

Yes. There are printed pieces on these pages. Some look like slides... or are they screenshots from well-designed websites? Were ANY of them made in PowerPoint? (I can feel you clutching your pearls.)

by Julie Terberg

by Julie Terberg

by Johanna Rehnvall

by Nolan Haims Creative

(You can probably guess where I'm going with this.)

15

Every. Single. One.

But using PPT is a pain in my ass.

I know. It's not an Adobe product, but PowerPoint has a surprisingly similar set of functions and abilities. Some are clunky, yes, but there are some tricks that any presentation designer worth their salt uses to work around that.

There's also a sizable chunk of stuff that it STILL doesn't do even after years of customers complaining about it. I still have hope.

That being said, grab your snack of choice and read on.

First thing's first: Let's speak the same language.

Shared language is important so you and I should probably have a chat. I want us to be on the same page in the same book, (metaphorically speaking since we already *literally* are).

Later on, we're going to have a ~~showcase~~ interface showdown. That's where I will point out any differences between what you might be used to and what PowerPoint serves up. Heads up, there is nothing labeled "kerning" or "leading" or "paragraph styles." (That last one is particularly painful.)

In the realm of presentation design, you'll hear people say things like "deck" and "prezo." I **hate** those terms. However, considering how many syllables "presentation" has in it, my ADHD is willing to overcome my dislike.

Throughout this book, when I mention a term that might mean something a little different from what you're used to, I'll make sure to point it out. Clarity is everything.

PowerPoint has a slight Mac vs. PC problem.

So... PowerPoint for Mac and PowerPoint for PC don't give you the same features. In some cases, a feature will exist in both versions but work completely differently. And I'm going to go out on a limb here and guess that many of you are hard-core Mac users. I'm sorry to say that PowerPoint on PC is FAR superior.

I highly recommend getting a license for Parallels so that you can run Windows on your Mac. It's a small investment for a more robust version of PowerPoint.

I made a handy-dandy little table of the features you might have trouble finding on a Mac. Keep in mind this list is as of August 17, 2024. Microsoft might update something and render part of this section completely OBE (overcome by events).

If something I cover in the rest of the book isn't available in either Mac or PC version, I'll let you know.

And thank you to both Nolan Haims and Jamie Garroch for being the ones who sussed this table out. I'm so happy I didn't have to do it myself. In fact, here are some QR codes that will take you straight to their articles.

Nolan's article

Jamie's article

Feature	PC	Mac
Home tab		
Reuse Slides	✓	
3D Model	✓	
Screen Recording	✓	
Reorder Objects		✓
Reorder Overlapping Objects		✓
Editing Group	✓	
Dictation	✓	
Insert tab		
Photo Album	✓	
Forms	✓	
Screen Recording	✓	
Draw tab		
Ruler	✓	
Track pad		✓
Design tab		
Custom Fonts	✓	
Animations tab		
Timeline view	✓	
In-ribbon Delay	✓	
Slide Show tab		
Alt+F5	✓	
Review tab		
Language	✓	
Compare	✓	
Reading Order pane	✓	
View tab		
Notes Pages / Layout	✓	
Color / Grayscale	✓	
Recording tab	✓	
Developer tab	✓	

Feature	PC	Mac
Video Format		
Insert Captions	✓	
Video Shape	✓	
Backstage view		
Info tab	✓	
Package for CD	✓	
Create Handouts	✓	
Publish to Microsoft Stream	✓	
Other		
blank.potx	✓	
Gridlines (not Guides)	✓	
Image Compression control	✓	
In-ribbon eyedropper	✓	
Video export to 4K	✓	
Video export to WMV	✓	
Video export to MOV	✓	✓
Save as theme file (thmx)	✓	
Save presentation as SVG/WMF/EMF	✓	
Save picture as SVG/WMF/EMF	✓	
Selection pane Alt+F10	✓	
Import Image (from device)	✓	✓
Capture Selection from Screen	✓	✓
Reapply Notes Master	✓	
Resize Presenter View Window	✓	
Import/Export QAT	✓	
Copy Paste Sections	✓	
Picture layouts in SmartArt	✓	

As of August 17, 2024.

You can be part of the secret club... The Insiders

I mean, if your place of work doesn't have your computers locked down more securely than Fort Knox, you can definitely be an insider. You get new features earlier than all the basic people. There IS a catch, though.

If you become an insider and you use a cool new feature and then you hand off the file to someone who isn't an insider, you might have issues. Nothing will be BROKEN, per se. For example, new transitions will fall back to simple fades. So how do you join? It's different on Mac vs. PC.

For my Mac-user friends:

1. Head up to that Help menu.
2. Choose "check for updates."
3. Choose "Advanced."
4. In the Update Channel, pick the one you want.

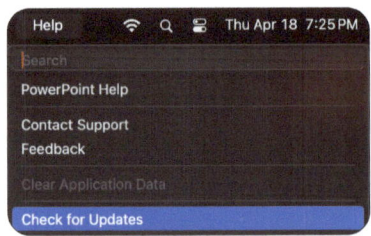

Current Channel: Regular old version most people use.

Current Channel (Preview): The first level of the special insider club.

Beta: Be an extreme insider.

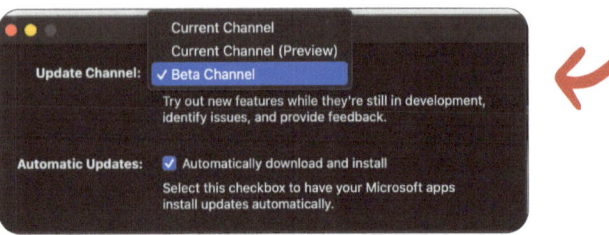

For my Windows friends:

1. Head over to the File tab.
2. Choose "Account" near the bottom.
3. Choose "Microsoft 365 Insider."
4. Choose "Change Channel."
5. Pick your poison.

It's also worth noting that you can hop between versions. You're not stuck with the preview or beta versions once you're there.

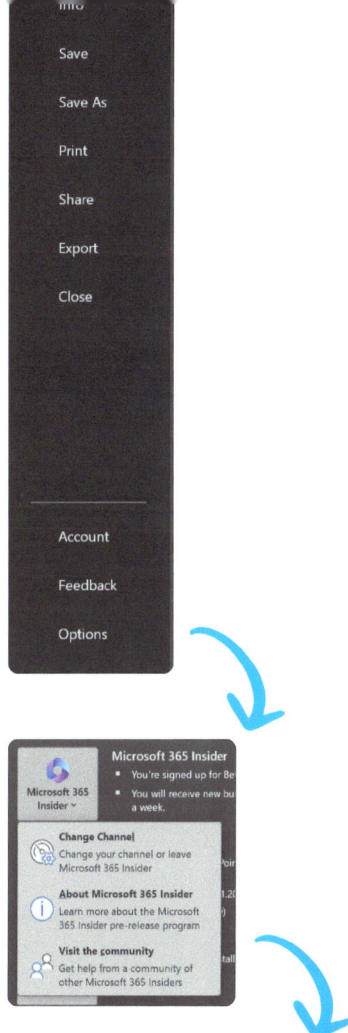

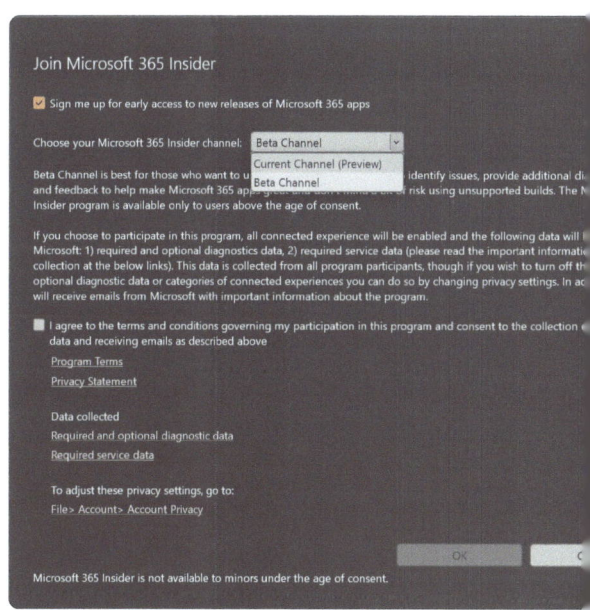

Get yourself familiar with PowerPoint's interface.

As I write this, I'm in the latest version of PowerPoint 365 circa August 2024. Yes, there will be updates after I publish this; however, the interface won't change all that much for the foreseeable future. (Of course, now that I've put that in writing, Microsoft will probably revolutionize PowerPoint and give us everything we ever wanted.)

Of course, there are differences between Mac and PC. You can set the interface color in each; however, Mac has fewer options.

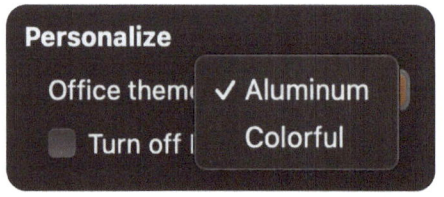

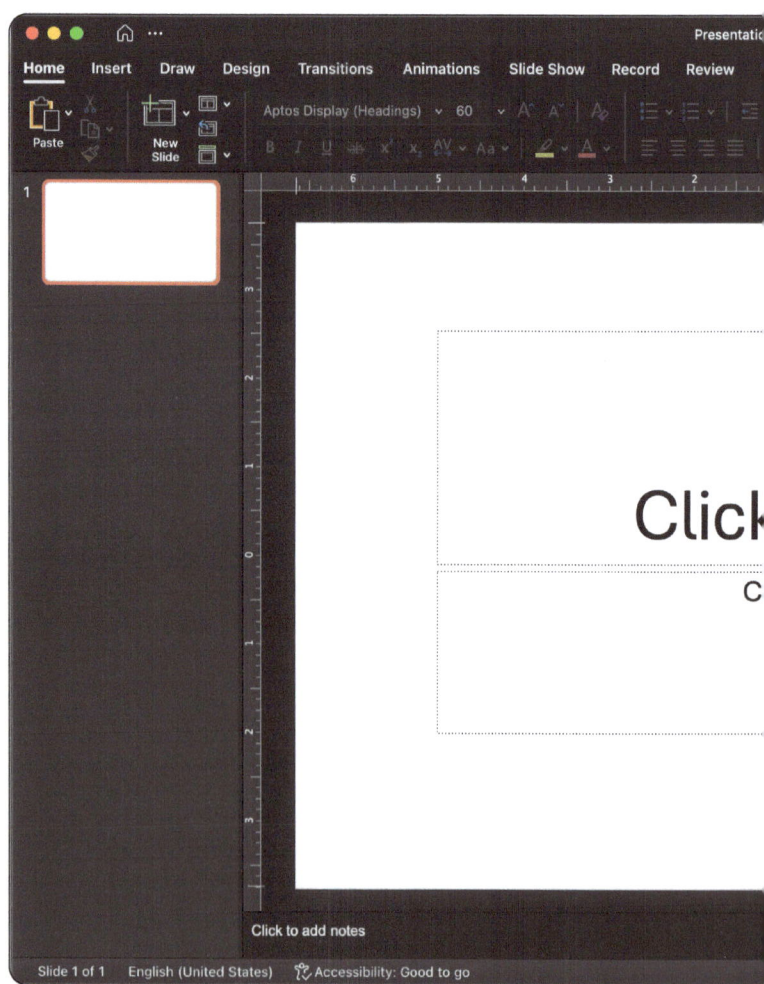

PC has a few more options than Mac does. What I find funny is how horrible PowerPoint looks if you change it to black. I use the darkest setting on Mac, but on PC? I use Dark Gray all day.

Fun fact: The black interface looks exceptionally horrible in Outlook.

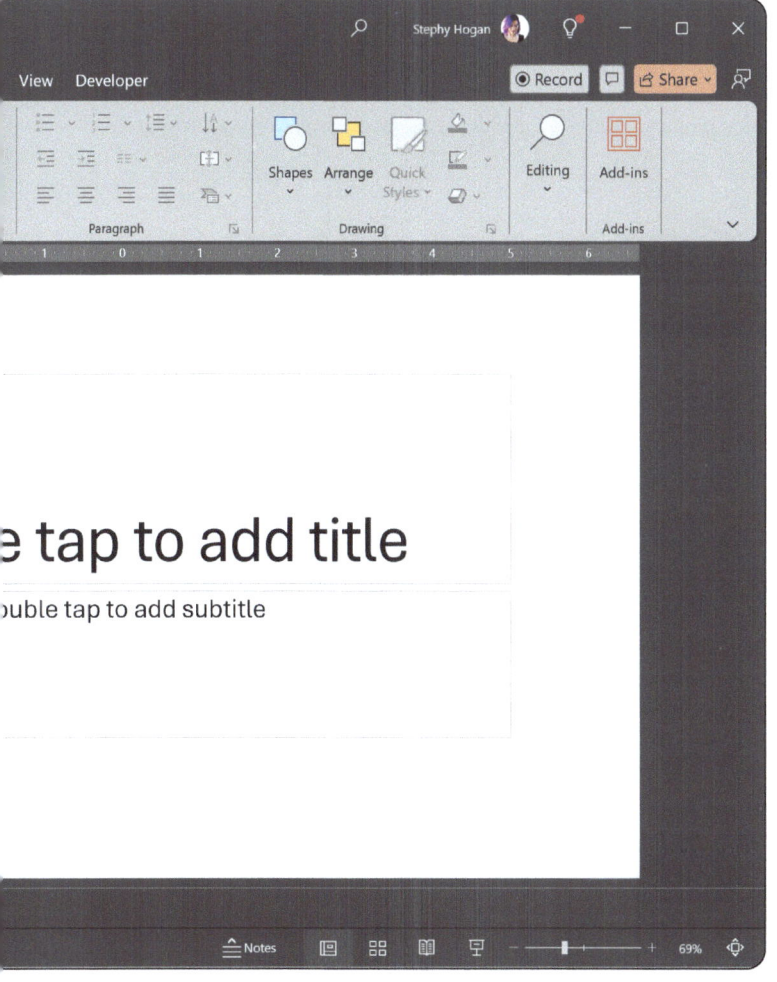

Check out the views...

If you've tried to avoid using PowerPoint like the plague, you might not know what secrets lie within the general user interface. Let's review.

Let's start with the Status Bar at the bottom, where there are buttons that zoom and change views. The normal view is what everyone thinks of when they think about PowerPoint. The slide sorter view is handy to see the overall flow and design consistency of a presentation. Reading view is one i always use to do a quick run through of my presentation (instead of slideshow mode) because I have an ultra *ultra*-wide screen monitor.

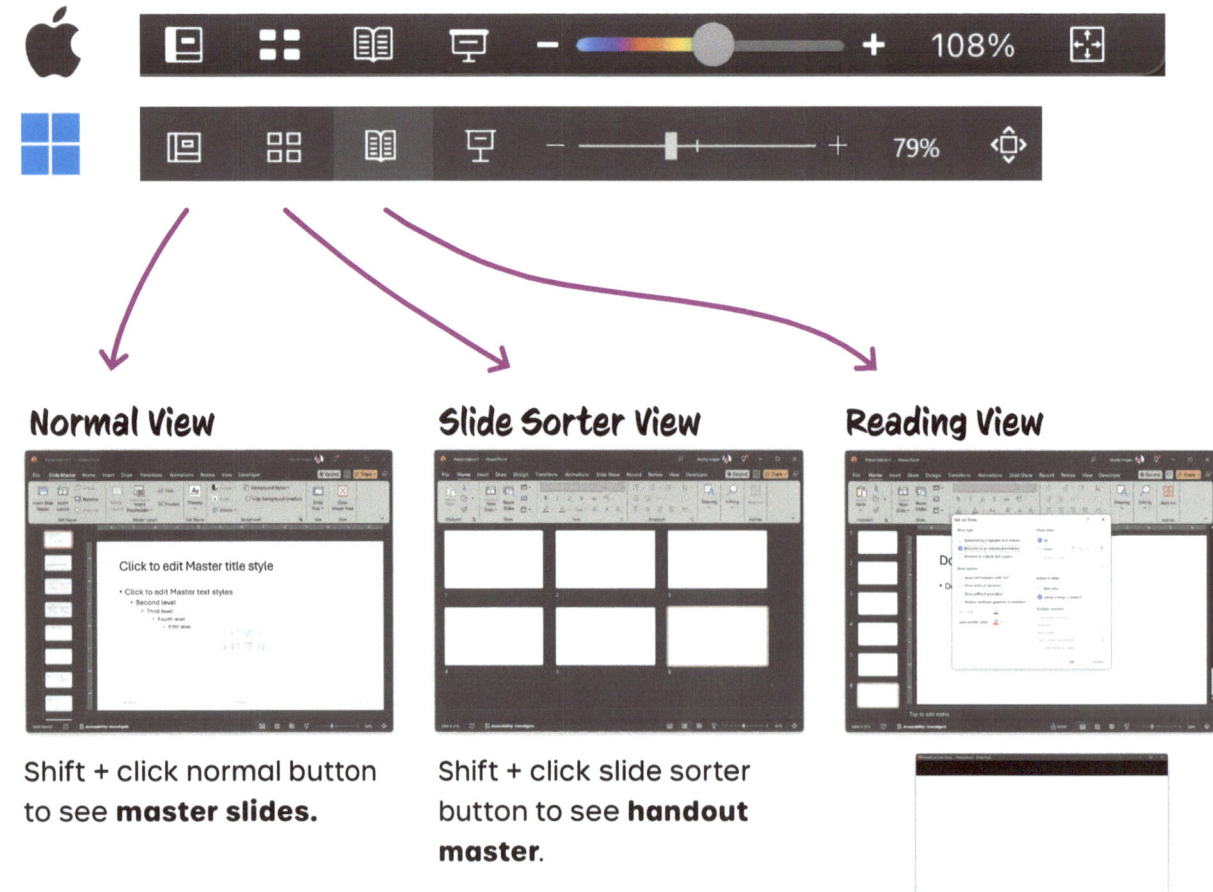

Normal View

Shift + click normal button to see **master slides.**

Slide Sorter View

Shift + click slide sorter button to see **handout master**.

Reading View

Master Slide and Layouts

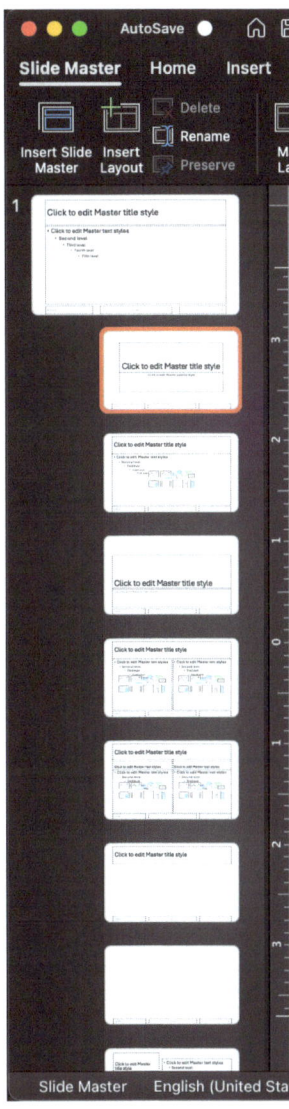
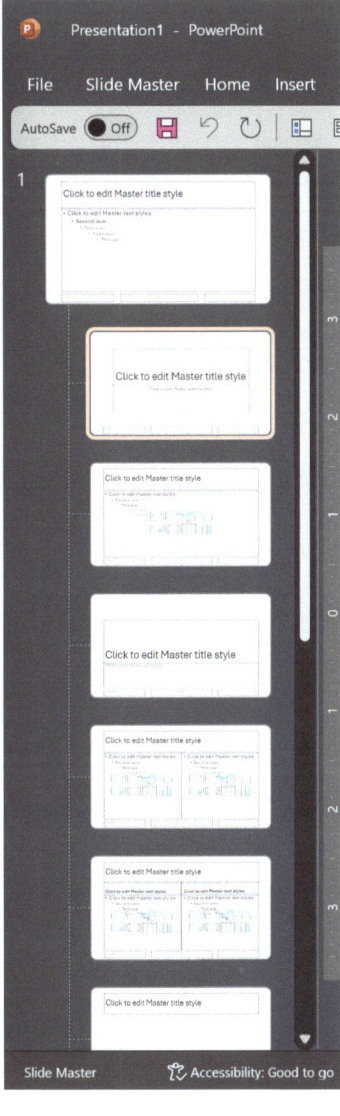

The slide master pane looks just about identical between Mac and PC.

Whatever you put on the parent slide will show on the child slides.

Worth noting: If you ever copy slides from one presentation into another, you'll most likely see many sets of slide parents and children. It can get really messy, really fast.

I am most DEFINITELY not going to talk about the intricacies of template creation. You want *this* book. Echo and Julie have written the bible on the topic.

Ribbons = Toolbars

The ribbon can be super useful—if you take a little time to customize it. Depending on what your screen size is and which platform you're working on, it can take up a LOT of real estate.

Sometimes it's so big, that you only see about 2/3rds of what's in it. Even on larger screens there will be times when you still can't find what you need.

Thankfully, you can customize it. Just right-click on any ribbon and choose "Customize Ribbon" and you'll get this beefy modal.

I recommend changing "Popular Commands" to "All Commands" and then go to town! Customize to your heart's content.

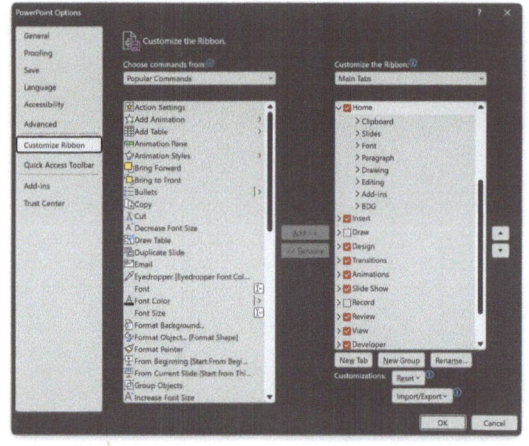

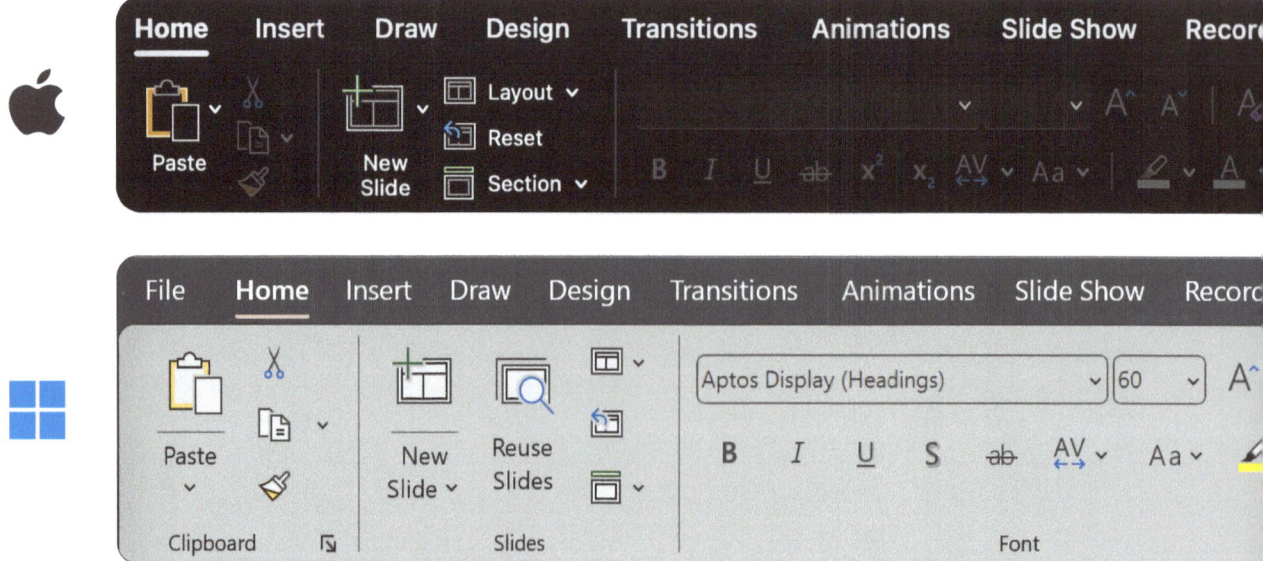

How many ribbons are there?

I'll bet you didn't think there were this many. These are all of the ribbons, both standard and contextual. And there are no repeats below. Seriously!

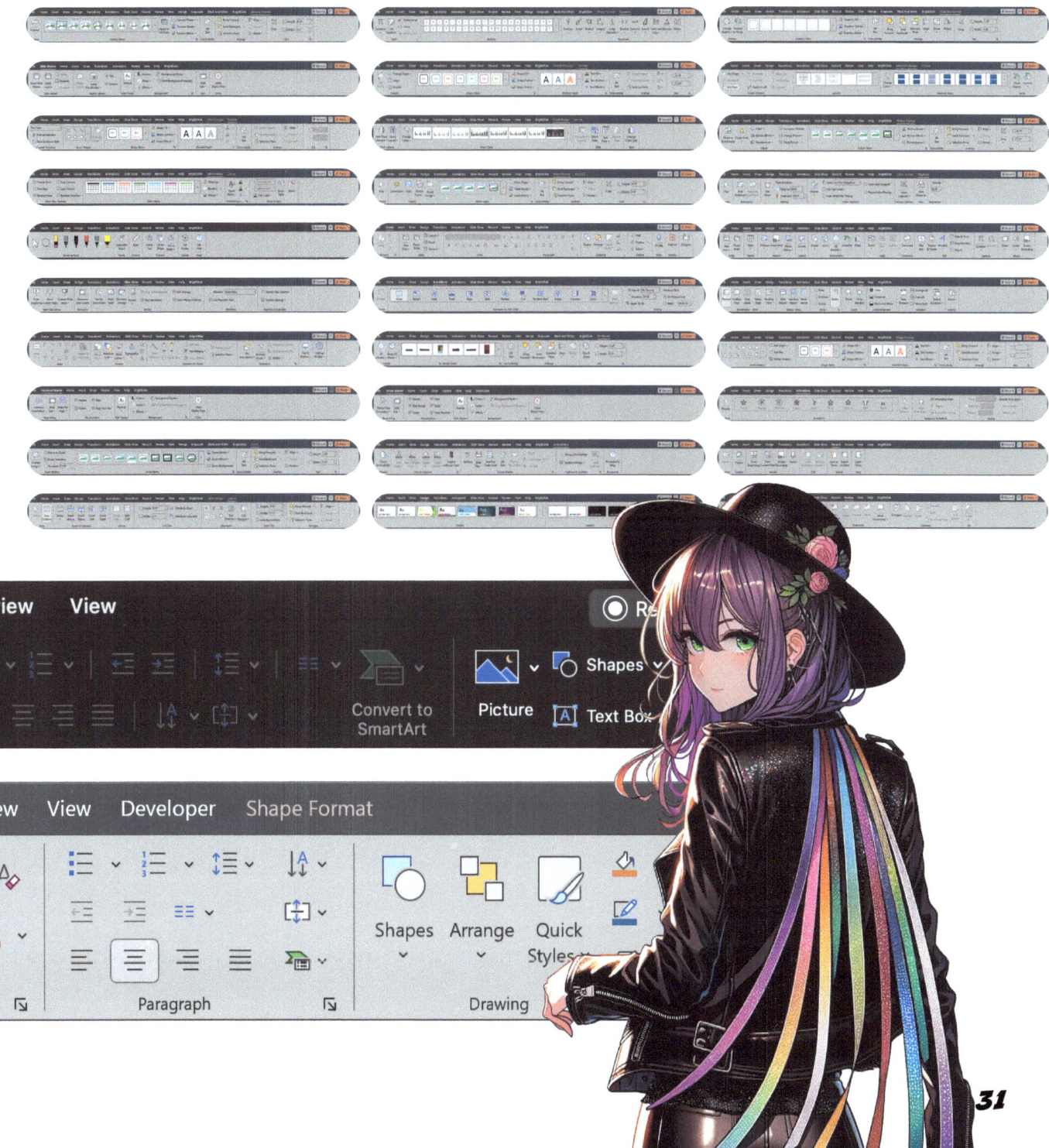

I've been looking for <enter tool name here> for way too long.

I know. Not many things are where you expect them to be. It doesn't help that there are 30ish different ribbons and just as many contextual panes.

Let's just go through the tools you're used to and where you can find them in PowerPoint. This will all be from the perspective of a PC user. (**I heard that audible gasp.** Or was it whining?) Good news is that 99% of it's the same in Mac.

I didn't actually do the math on that, so don't come at me if the number isn't really 99%.

Slide Setup

I suppose it makes sense to start with setting up your slides the way you would a new document (if you use Creative Suite). Did you know you can make custom sized slides (even make a printed poster).

Slide Size

You may be used to:

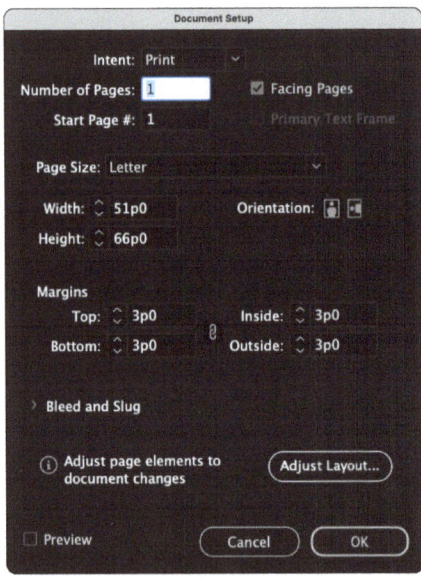

What PowerPoint offers:

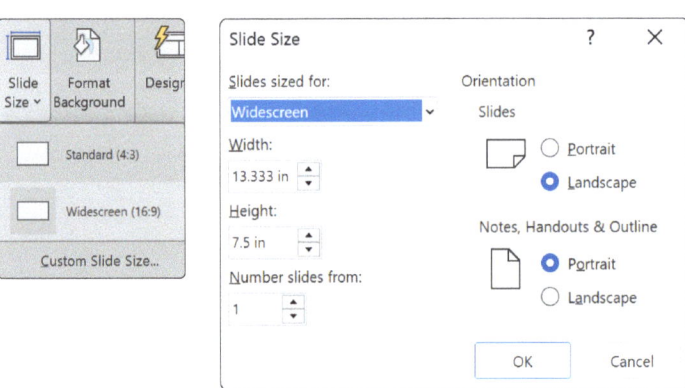

InDesign asks you how you want to set up your document when you first hit "New." PowerPoint does not. For most people, that's fine. But sometimes I want to mix things up a bit and NOT use the default settings.

So if **you** want to change the slide size, you can head to the **Home Ribbon > Slide Size > Custom Slide Size**.

You might notice something weird: the actual dimensions of a widescreen presentation is not 16 in by 9 in.

It's 13.333 in by 7.5 in.

Yeah. I'm with you. WHY?!

Guides & Grids

You may be used to:

Just dragging guides onto the artboard. Sadly, you can't do that in PowerPoint.

And even though I KNOW that, it doesn't stop me from accidentally trying to drag a new guide onto the slide.

What PowerPoint offers:

You can turn guides, grids, and rulers on in the **View Ribbon**.

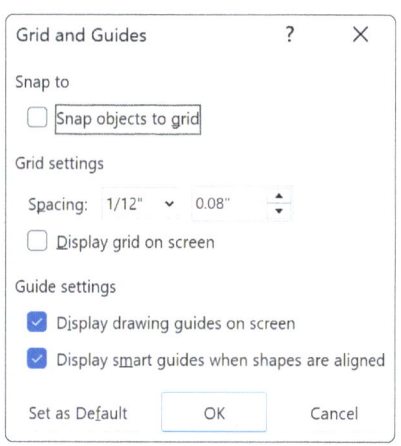

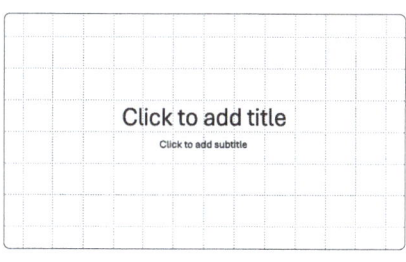

You can adjust their settings as well. Personally, I never use the grid but I always used guides.

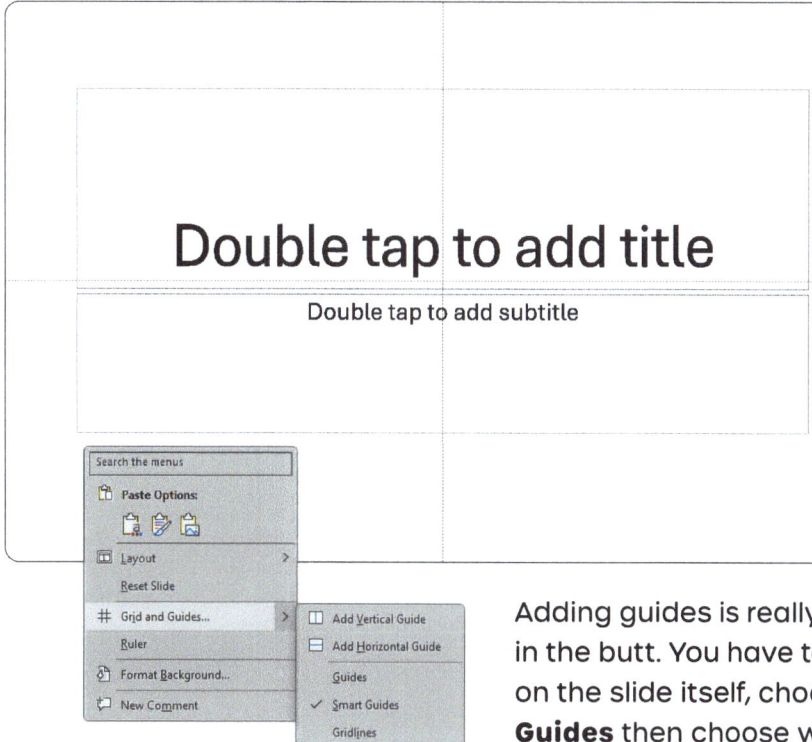

Adding guides is really quite a pain in the butt. You have to right-click on the slide itself, choose **Grids and Guides** then choose whatever you want from there. It's dumb.

Align & Distribute

You may be used to:

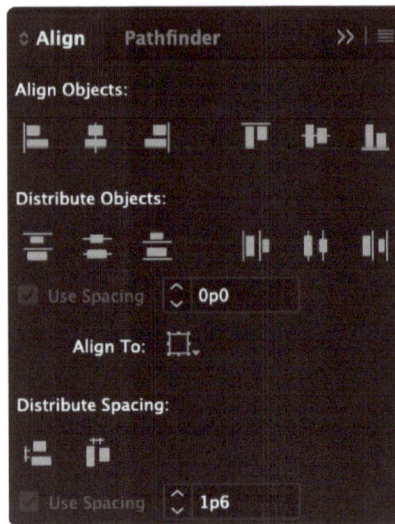

What PowerPoint offers:

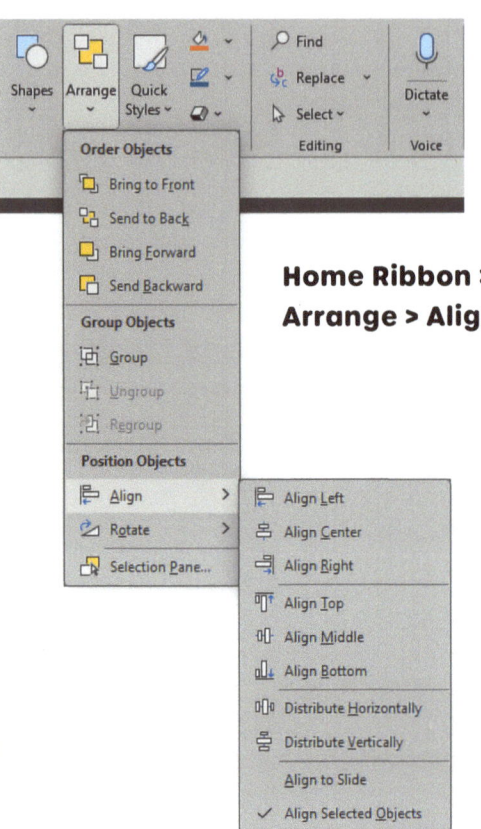

Home Ribbon > Arrange > Align

Happy day! The same align and distribute options that you're used to are in PowerPoint as well. What's sad is that they aren't in a nice docked pane. I'll teach you how to work around that on page 108. However, you can't choose an anchor point to align to.

Rotate & Flip

You may be used to:

What PowerPoint offers:

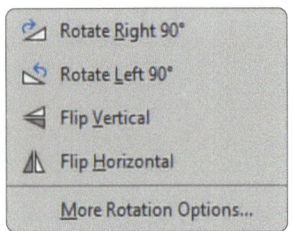

In that same location as above, choose **Rotate** and you'll have access to flipping as well. Woo. hoo.

Layout Helpers

You may be used to:

Manual labor. These are things you're probably used to doing by hand.

PowerPoint offers you Smart Art & Picture Layouts (which are the same thing, actually) and are used to automatically layout photos, org charts, cycles—all kinds of stuff.

By default, they're fairly ugly. Designers hate them. But I was once told by a smart human to think of it as Smart *Start* instead of Smart Art.

Use it to jump start the layout you want to create, then **ungroup it twice** and you can edit to your heart's content.

Smart Art is on the **Insert Ribbon**.

Picture Layout is on the **Picture Format Ribbon** (select your images first).

What PowerPoint offers:

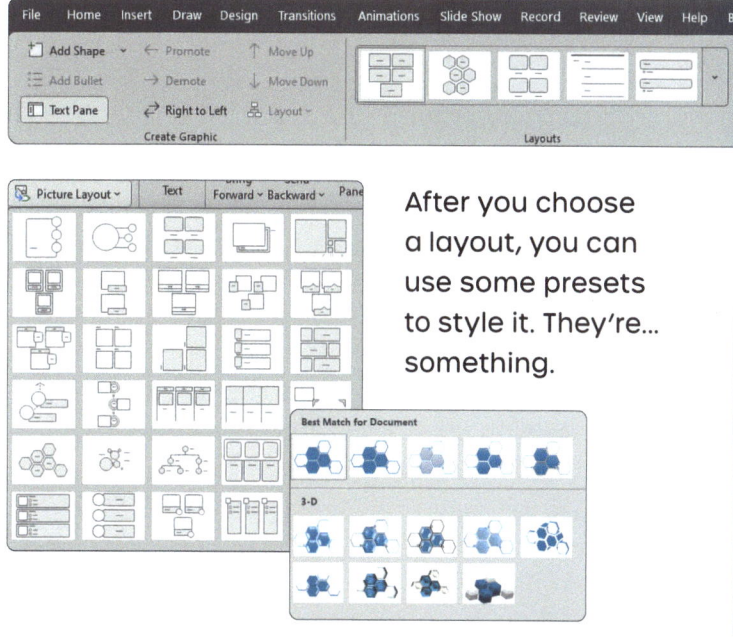

After you choose a layout, you can use some presets to style it. They're… something.

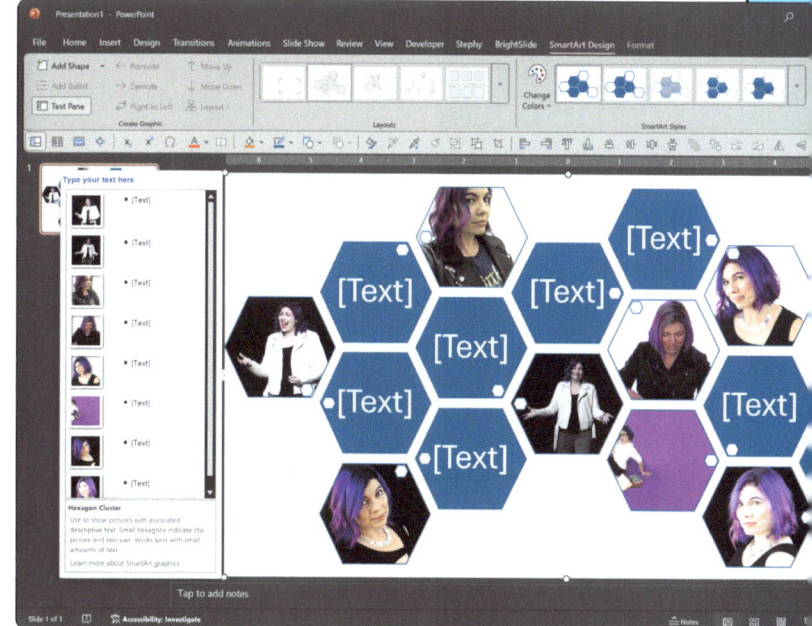

Typography

You may have noticed that there are no paragraph styles in PowerPoint. Yes, Word has styles. You would think that because both are part of the Microsoft suite, PowerPoint would have paragraph styles as well. It's been a point of annoyance in the presentation community since forever. (There's no text wrap or text frame linking either.)

I love InDesign. I'm using it right now. There's oh SO MUCH control over how this text appears. PowerPoint has fewer options, but it's not all *that* bad.

Just remember that when you have placeholders or regular text frames, you might want to change the text fit to **Do Not Fit**. Just right-click on your text object, choose **Format Object > Text Options > Text Box > Do not Autofit.**

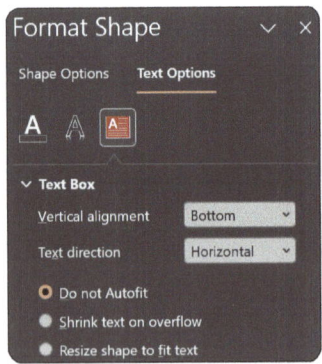

There are two categories of fonts you can use: safe fonts and everything else. Safe fonts are the ones that show by default in your font dropdown.

You want to use safe fonts. Trust me. Why? Because those fonts will look the same on all computers.

If you use a font from "everything else" and the person you hand off your presentation to doesn't have that font on their Machine, it'll show up as the default theme font. If the default theme font is an "everything else" font, text will default to Aptos or Helvetica. Your leading might not be the same. CEOs don't like it. Ask me how I know.

You can embed fonts but that's no guarantee that there won't be issues.

 You can learn all about safe fonts from my friend Julie Terberg. Use this QR code to go to her guide.

Aptos humor...

I would be remiss if I didn't share one of my favorite creators, Elle Cordova. Aptos reminded me of her. This QR code goes to her reel about Aptos. You're welcome.

POST SHARED ON JANUARY 29
BY ELLECORDOVA

38

Font Settings

To get here, you use the little dialogue launcher in the bottom right of the Font section. A lot of stuff is a repeat from what's directly in the ribbon, but there are a couple of things you can only access using this dialogue.

What PowerPoint offers:

You may be used to:

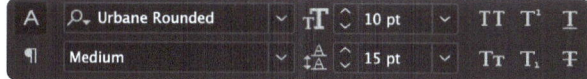

Alignment

You might be used to:

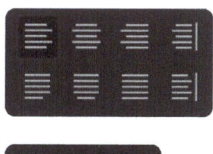

What PowerPoint offers:

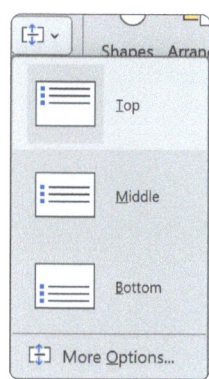

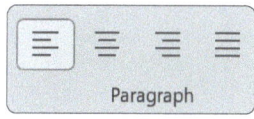

You don't get left-, center-, right-, or vertical-justified options. That's OK. You don't need them anyway.

Honestly, unless you're designing text art, please never use any kind of justified text. Ew.

Text Wrap

You might be used to:

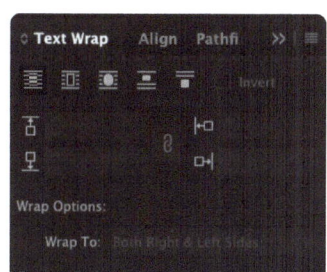

What PowerPoint offers:

Nothing. Nothing at all. No text wrap.

Yeah, I know how you feel.

Bullets & Numbering

You might be used to:

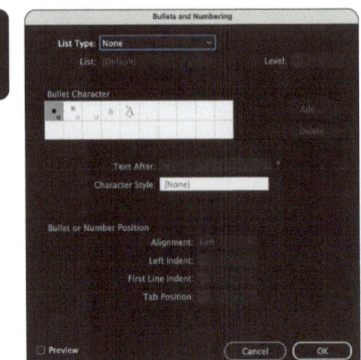

Bullets & numbering will probably drive you a little batty. Once a presentation is handed around a few times, the styles get all janky. Be prepared to reset the slide and reformat by hand.

You can customize the bullets a little bit if you choose **Home > Bullets/Numbering > Bullets and Numbering**.

Then if you choose **Customize**, you're able to choose a different glyph from a different font, color, and size.

What PowerPoint offers:

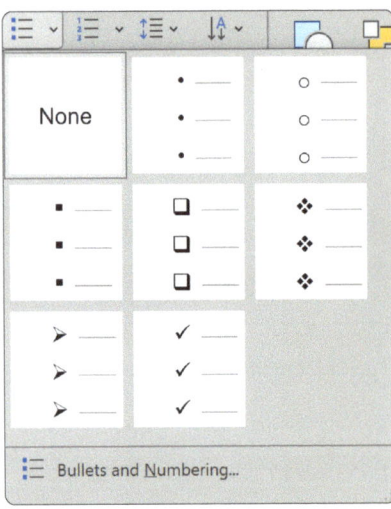

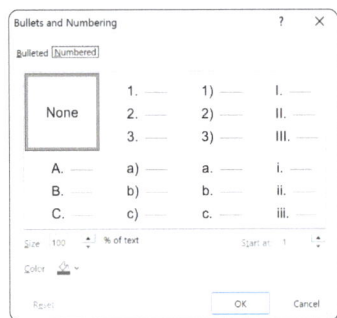

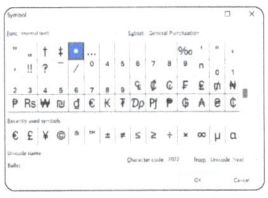

Columns

You may be used to:

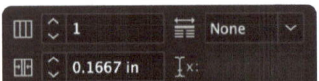

What PowerPoint offers:

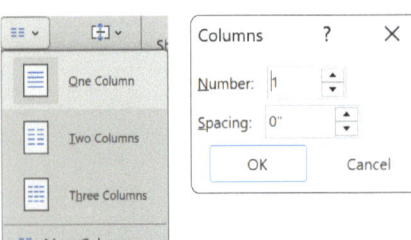

I don't think people use columns enough in their presentations. It's a shame that we can't span or split columns, but that's a minor pain. So I'm OK with it. You'll find columns in the **Home Ribbon**.

Find Fonts

Replacing Fonts

You might think, after hours of careful design and review, that you have only used 2 typefaces. Funny thing is, there will always be more than you think (bullets are usually the culprit).

There can also be times when you get weird font warnings when you open a file.

If you want to see a list of all of the fonts in your presentation, there IS a way to do it and you can even replace fonts. How?

Go to **Edit > Find > Replace Fonts**.

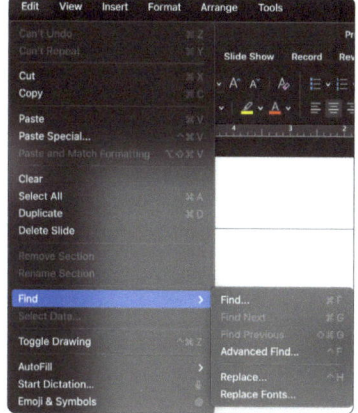

Glyphs

You may be used to:

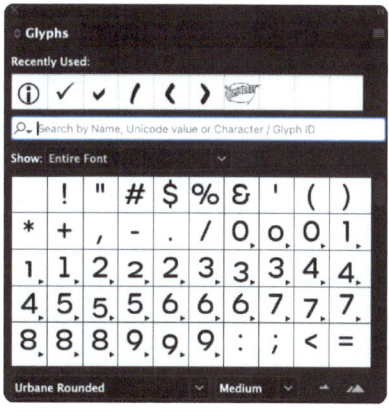

I'm sure the only reason glyphs are called **Symbols** in PowerPoint is because of the type of person who uses the program (typically NOT designers). However, "symbol" isn't quite right to me. You don't get just symbols—you see all of the glyphs in that font.

What PowerPoint offers:

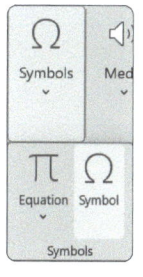
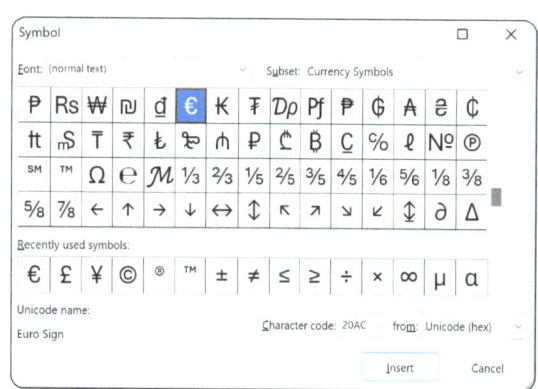

What I think is neat in PowerPoint is that they also give you the unicode for each glyph. Because I'm a nerd like that.

41

Leading & Indents

You may be used to:

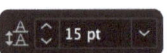

What PowerPoint offers:

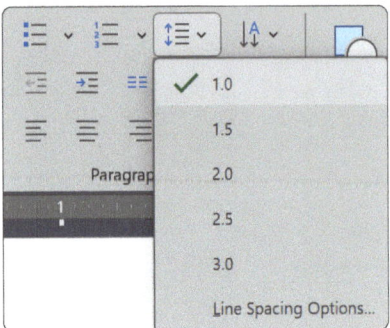

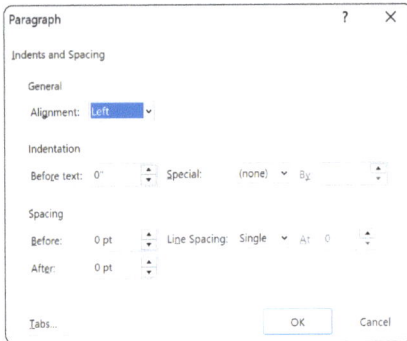

PowerPoint calls leading "line spacing."

Yes, it looks very basic. Don't worry, those aren't all of your choices. (These are sIlly default choices. I mean, who on earth triple spaces things?)

Unless I'm using 1.0, I always go into **Line Spacing Options**. I prefer to do the "multiply" option, and setting it anywhere between 0.9 and 1.3.

And look! There are some other spacing and indent things in that modal! How handy.

Kerning & Tracking

You might be used to:

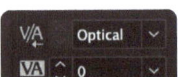

What PowerPoint offers:

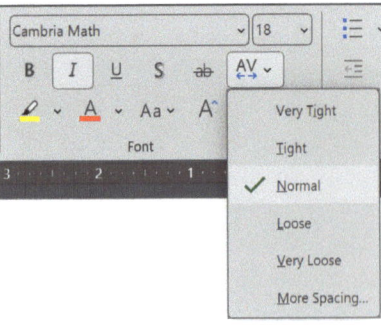

We call it **Character Spacing** in here. You've got a little wiggle room with tracking (but not kerning). If you want better control, install BrightSlide.

Y'all. Look at the size of this modal when you choose "More Spacing." I like white space, but that's a bit much.

Text Case

You may be used to:

What PowerPoint offers:

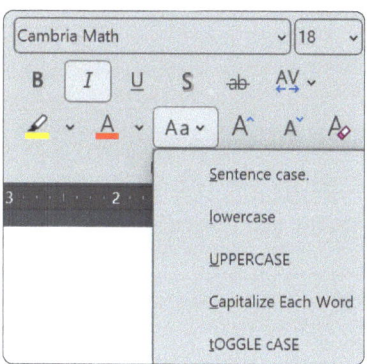

Fairly self-explanatory except for that "tOGGLE cASE" one. It'll make all lower-case letters into upper-case letters and vice versa. Why? I dunno. If you have a use case for it, Tell me on LinkedIn.

Text Direction

You may be used to:

This exists in one place in InDesign: tables. You'll see more on this in the Tables section.

What PowerPoint offers:

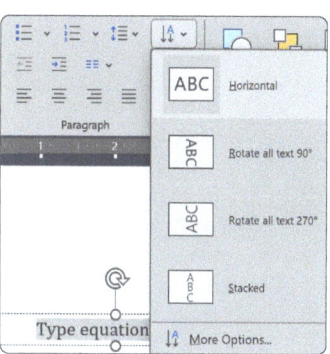

Here's another one that I feel is silly for the most part. If I want my text rotated, I'll rotate the text box. OK, maybe I'll use it in a table.

The "Stacked" option, however could be useful! I like that it's there.

Tabs

You may be used to:

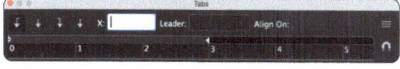

What PowerPoint offers:

I'm pretty sure not a lot of people know about this. PowerPoint lets you do all the tab types that InDesign does. Just click on the TINY tabs button to change the type. Just make sure you have rulers turned on (it's in the view tab).

Color

This isn't about color correction. We'll get into that later. In this section, you'll learn all the weird ways color is automatically applied to different things and where color choices are depending on what you're doing.

Be prepared. Color swatches are EVERYWHERE. It's not like in the Creative Suite where you have ONE panel to set fill and stroke colors on whatever you've selected.

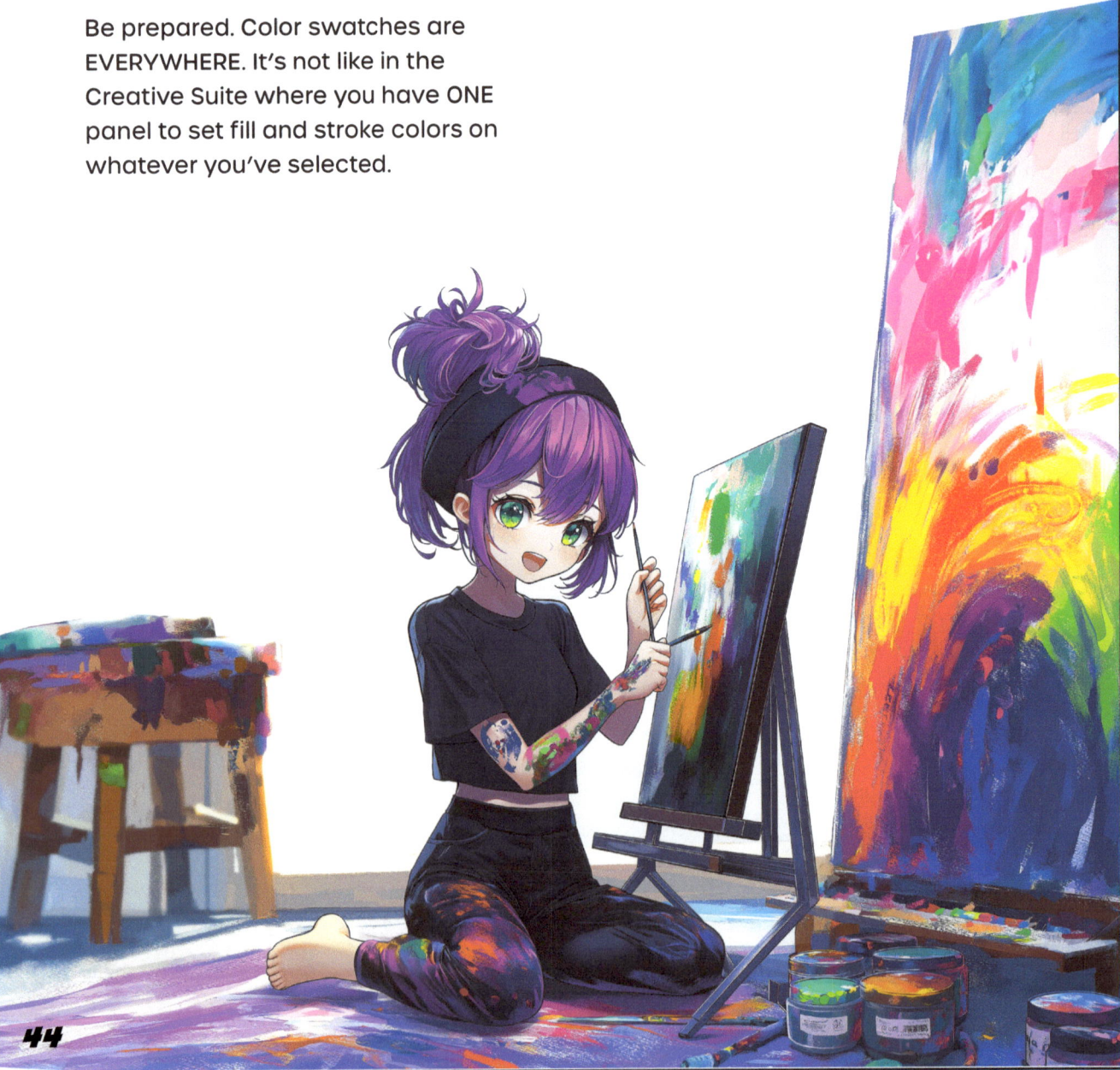

Swatches

You may be used to:

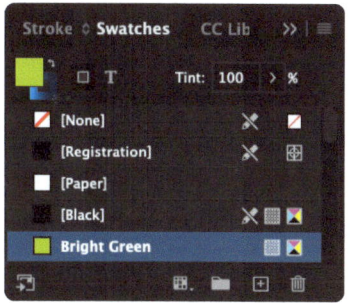
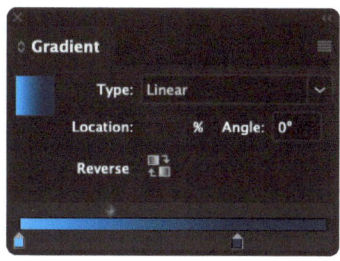

What PowerPoint offers:

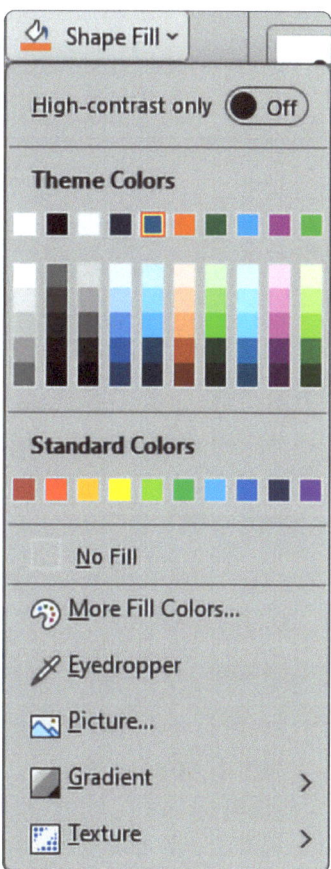

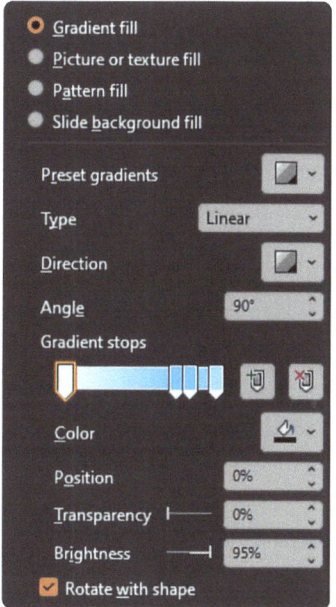

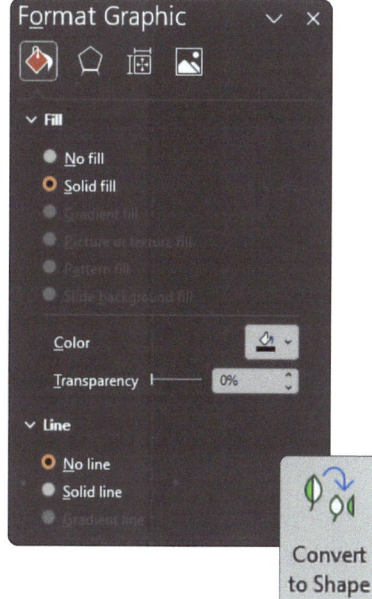

You'll get a deep dive into this thing on the next page. You'll see this same dropdown almost everywhere color is involved.

Gradients are pretty decent too. The only thing that stinks is that you can't save custom gradient swatches.

This one is a little odd. When you insert an icon from the ribbon, it's called a "graphic." And you can't fill graphics with gradients, pictures, textures, or the slide background. To do that, you have to use the **Convert to Shape** button.

45

Anatomy of the Color Picker

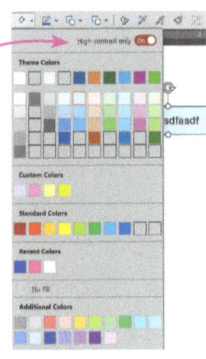 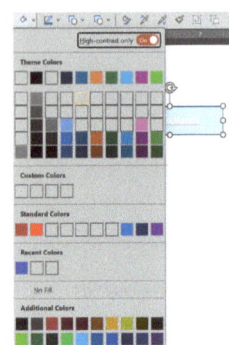

For dark text.   For light text.

Keep your slides accessible.
Select a text box or shape with text in it and turn this on. It'll show you (in this case) fill colors that contrast enough with the text contained in it. (It's a super cool features not found in Adobe Products.)

Light 1, Dark 1, Light 2, Dark 2
Each pair contains the default slide background and text colors.

Accent Colors 1 to 6
Used to automatically color shapes, lines, charts, word art, tables, & smart art.

Tints & Shades
Sooooooo...PowerPoint isn't the best at making proper tints & shades. They've gotten better, but be very intentional when using them.

Custom Colors
If you need to add extra colors to your file/template, you can. It's easy! (On PC side if you have BrightSlide.)

There's a convoluted workaround on Mac, but I'm not going to teach you that.

Instead, go buy my friends' template building book.

Microsoft Chose These
Just ye olde standard, slightly expanded rainbow. I occasionally use these to color text that I know I'll have to change later. Another set of absolute colors.

Colors You Manually Chose (instead of using this dropdown)
Also known as "absolute" colors because if you change themes, objects that use these colors will remain the same.

Chart Colors

You may be used to:

Yeah... Illustrator charts STILL suck after 20 years, there's no other way to say it. If you need high res charts for print, make them in PowerPoint first, right click on it, and choose "Save as Picture."

You'll get a PNG.

With a transparent background.

And it'll be 330ppi!

See? PowerPoint **is** cool.

What PowerPoint offers:

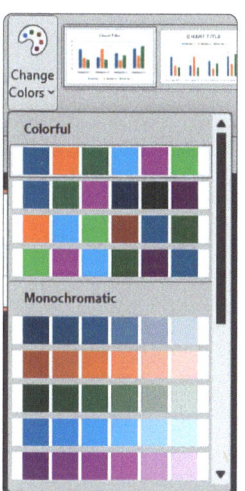

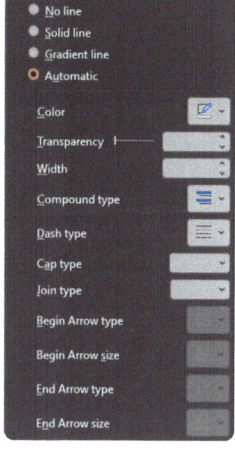

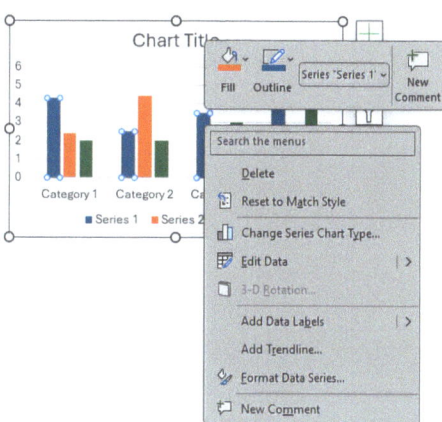

You can change the color of all parts of a chart just by selecting each piece, right-clicking and either change it there or choose **Format [chart part]**.

Highlighter Color

You may be used to:

...using fancy underlines to act as a highlighter.

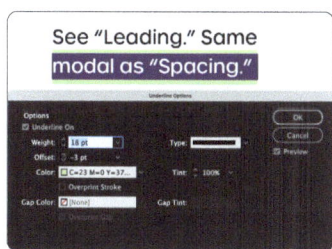

What PowerPoint offers:

There's an actual highlight feature! It looks like the example below about Pixel. The issue I have with it is that PowerPoint gives you typical real-world highlighter colors and YOU CAN'T CHANGE THEM. Boo.

<mark>Pixel</mark> is the best dog ever.

Slide Fill

What PowerPoint offers:

Obviously, Adobe doesn't have an equivalent to this. Something worth noting—if you think you can set the background as transparent and export an image of the slide with a transparent background, you can't. It's a real bummer.

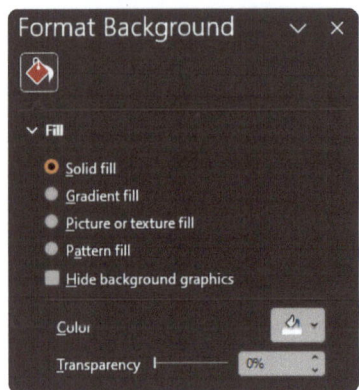

Table Colors

You may be used to:

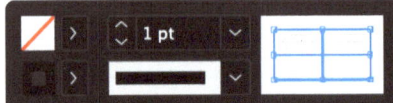

What PowerPoint offers:

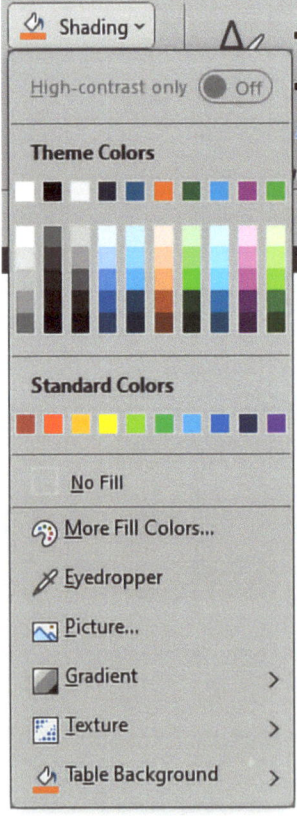

We'll get into tables a little more later. I just want to mention here that while cell fill is called **Shading** like you're used to, border colors are NOT called "border colors." Instead, it's called **Pen Color**.

And I think that's just silly.

Theme Colors

You may be used to:

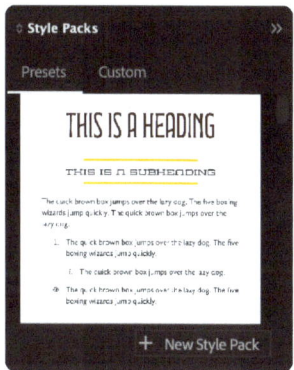

What PowerPoint offers:

I've already given you a ton of detailed info about colors from themes. But I haven't covered variants yet.

You'll find them in the **Design Tab next to Themes**. From left to right, the background colors are Light 1, Light 2, Dark 1 and Dark 2. Accent colors stay the same.

Know what that means?

Make sure your accent colors contrast enough with both your light and dark background colors if you're building your own theme.

Vector Stuff

PowerPoint's vector tools will be a pleasant surprise for anyone coming from the Adobe world. Sure, it's not Illustrator, but it gets the job done when you need to whip up something clean and scalable without switching programs. So, while you might not be creating the next Mondrian, you'll definitely find it's capable enough to keep your slides looking sharp.

Pen Tool

You may be used to:

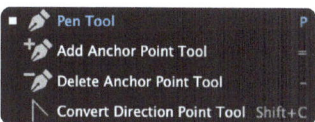

What PowerPoint offers:

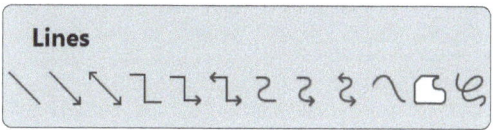

PowerPoint *does* have something equivalent to the pen tool, but you would NEVER know it by looking at it. They're hidden in the **Shapes** dropdown.

No, really! I swear! See the curve tools up there? Those are pen-like tools. And the silly white shape? THAT is your pen tool.

You can even modify existing shapes like you can in Illustrator.

Add points
Click the shape outline while pressing Ctrl.

Delete points
Click the point while pressing Ctrl.

Smooth points
Convert to smooth points by pressing **Shift** while dragging either of the handles attached to the point.

Straight points
Convert to straight points by pressing **Ctrl** while dragging either of the handles attached to the point.

Corner points
Convert to corner points by pressing **Alt** while dragging either of the handles attached to the point.

Clipping Masks

You may be used to:

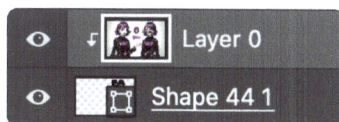

What PowerPoint offers:

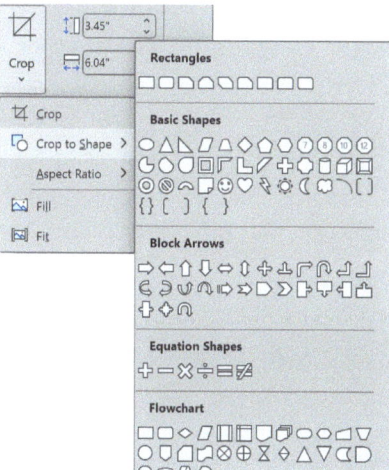

They aren't called clipping masks. It's called "Crop to Shape." You have to pick from the shape dropdown options.

OR...you can put a picture on the slide, make any shape over it and use the **Merge Shapes** (page 58) tool to make a clipping mask effect.

51

Shapes

You may be used to:

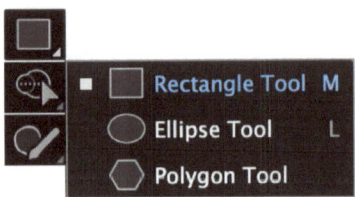

 And, well, basically just Illustrator in general.

What PowerPoint offers:

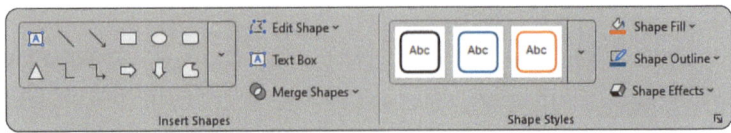

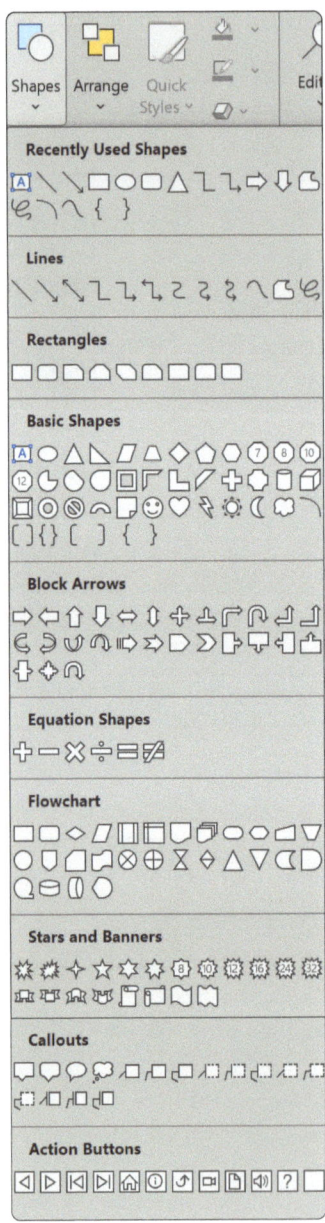

On the **Home** and **Insert Ribbons** is where you'll find Shapes.

And there are a LOT of them. A rather silly amount. I've only ever used a dozen or so—maybe a little more.

By using the callout boxes, you can work around the fact that there are no paragraph rules in PowerPoint. I'll tell you about it later.

Shapes have their own contextual ribbon. You'll probably use it mostly for the "Merge Shapes" tool (better known as Pathfinder).

Pathfinder

You may be used to:

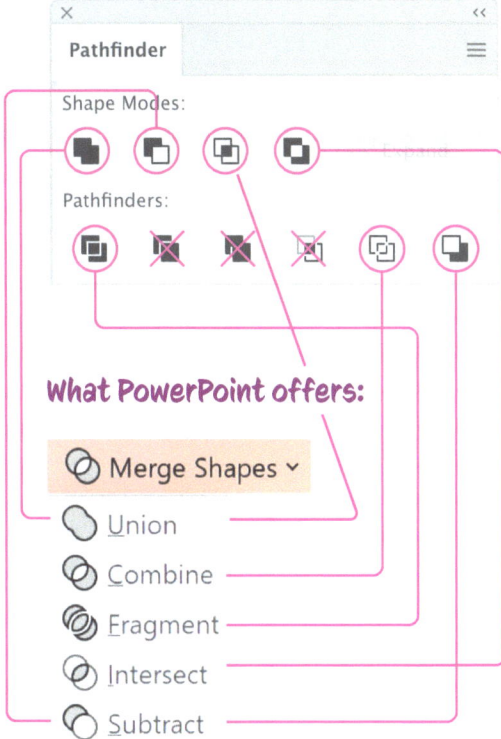

What PowerPoint offers:

Illustrator's Pathfinder gives you loads of handy tools to make custom shapes with and PowerPoint has all but 3 of them. It's called **Merge Shapes** and it's in the **Shape Format contextual ribbon**.

I'm OK with not having 3 of them. I always HATED messing with compound paths. Especially in other people's messy files.

Illustrator:	PowerPoint:
1. Unite	1. Unite
2. Minus Front	2. Subtract
3. Minus Back	3. Subtract
4. Intersect	4. Intersect
5. Exclude	5. Combine
6. Divide	6. Fragment
7. Trim	7. N/A
8. Merge	8. N/A
9. Crop	9. N/A
10. Outline	10. Combine + no fill + stroke

Original Shapes

Results

 AI: Unite
PPT: Union

 AI: Divide
PPT: Fragment

 AI: Minus Front
PPT: Subtract

 AI: Exclude
PPT: Combine

 AI: Intersect
PPT: Intersect

 AI: Minus Back
PPT: Subtract

 AI: Exclude
PPT: Combine + no fill + stroke (or just… leave out the combine part and group instead)

Icons

Icons are a little different from shapes.

Unlock all formatting options: **Graphics Format Ribbon > Convert to Shape**

I've already mentioned this in swatches, but I'll repeat it in case you're skipping around.

When you insert an icon from the ribbon, it's called a "graphic." And you can't fill graphics with gradients, pictures, textures, or the slide background. To do that, you have to use the **Convert to Shape** button.

Lines & Strokes

You may be used to:

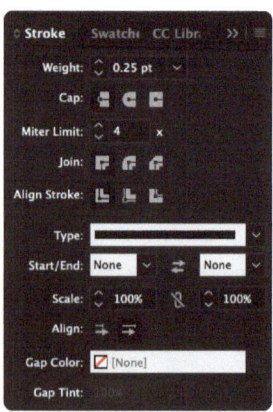

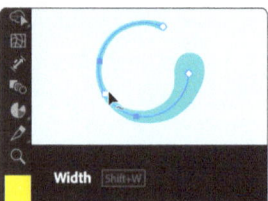

What PowerPoint offers:

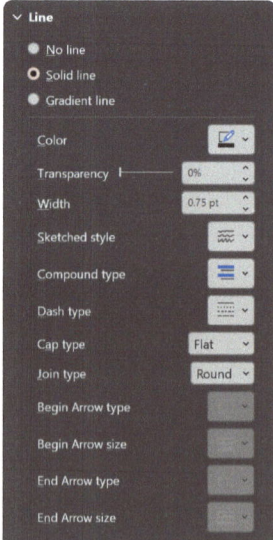

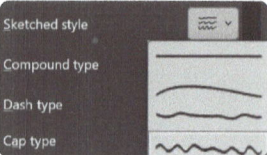

If you've spent any amount of time in Illustrator, you've probably played with variable strokes, different brushes, and all kinds of other fun things.

Sadly, we don't have those options in PowerPoint. All is not lost, though! There's a thing called **Sketchy Style**.

Sketchy outlines are fun. You can find the option under **Line** in the **Format Pane**. But they don't work on lines—just shapes.

Weird.

54

Text to Outline

You may be used to:

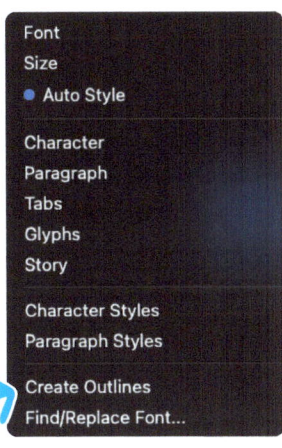

What PowerPoint offers:

Nothing. Not natively, anyway. But I'll show you a trick. Remember two pages ago when I showed you PowerPoint's version of pathfinder? We can use **Merge Shapes** with a shape-text pair.

For example, if you have a big rectangle shape and a text box on top of it, you can select them both and choose **Intersect**. Voila! Outlined text!

And since it matters which you select first, I'll pass along this brilliant tip from my friend Mike Parkinson:

First, select the cookie dough.

Then select the cookie cutter.

Mike says, "You're welcome."

Ohhhhhhh crop.

Hehehe. Classic design joke. I know it's not funny, but give a girl a break. I've been staring at this screen for weeks. Let's talk crop.

PowerPoint Location

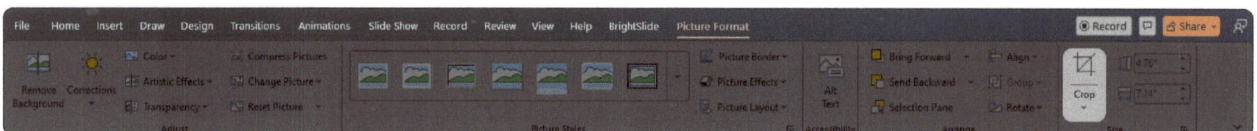

Select your picture, then: **Picture Format Tab > Crop**

I wanted to talk about **Fit** and **Fill** on the next page AFTER I talked about crop to shape and stuff, but I have a lot to say and it won't fit over there.

You can crop to proportionally **fit** the whole image in the shape you put it in—or crop it to **fill** the whole shape.

Content and Picture Placeholders will automatically either crop to fit or fill itself with your chosen image. Each one acts differently and you should be aware of it..

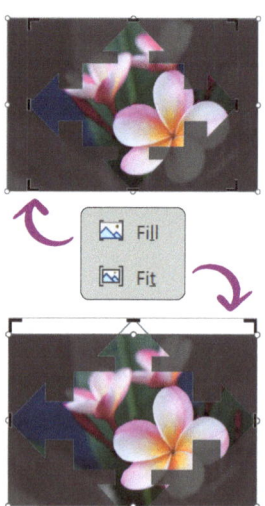

Content Placeholders
- Photos fit the **larger** dimension of the picture.
- The placeholder will shrink to fit the smaller dimension.

You always see the entire photo, but the layout varies between slides.

Picture Placeholders
- Photos fit the **smaller** dimension to the placeholder.
- Then the photo will be cropped in the other dimension.

The layout stays constant, but part of the picture may not be visible.

Cropping Photos

You may be used to:

What PowerPoint offers:

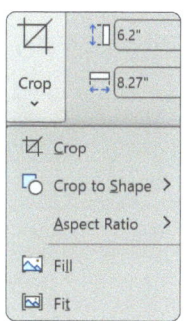

There are some pretty decent ways to crop in PowerPoint. Yes, there's regular cropping, but there's also **Crop to Shape** which is essentially a clipping mask tool. And you can **Crop to Ratios**, as well. (You can't do custom ratios like in Photoshop, but this is still pretty awesome.)

Crop to Shape

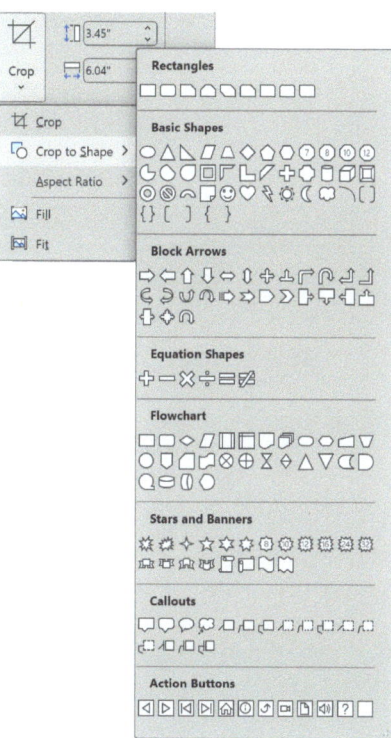

Crop to Aspect Ratio

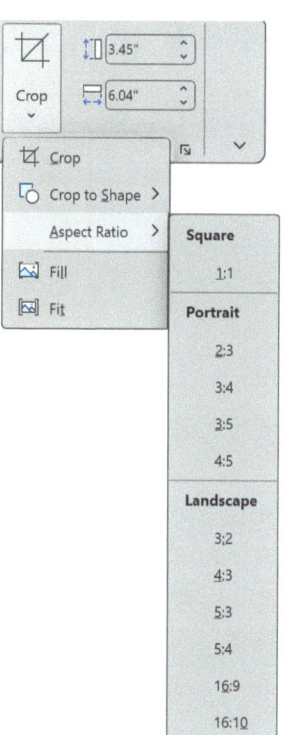

Cropping Video

A quick note about cropping video. You might discover that when you right-click on a video there is no crop option listed. That doesn't mean you can't. You have to choose the **Video Format Ribbon** to access cropping.

Go to **Video Tools > Format Tab**, then click **Video Shape > Oval** (or other desired shape).

Photo Editing

OK, between you and me, I don't edit photos in PowerPoint at all. I use Photoshop for everything but cropping. However, there's a surprising amount of stuff you can do directly in PowerPoint—some of it I actually like.

You may be used to:

I'm not going to bother picking out specific Photoshop tools just to keep up with my pattern of "You may be used to" and "What PowerPoint offers." I might as well screenshot the whole program. Instead, you get the app icon.

PowerPoint Location

Select your picture, then: **Picture Format Ribbon**

Quick Tip: Compression

If your presentation file size is too big, you can compress your pictures. Just know that if you use this tool, the Reset tool won't have any effect on the pictures you compressed.

Quick Tip: Reset

If you've played with your photos too much and you just want to start over, don't bother with "undo." Just hit the reset button.

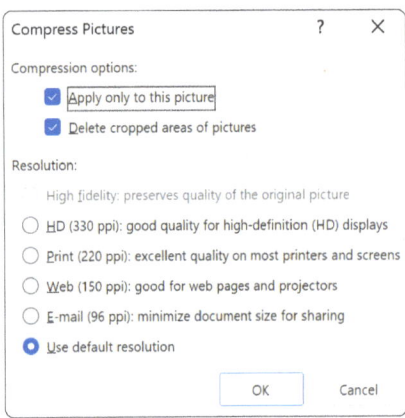

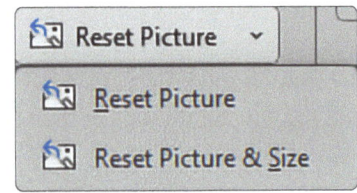

58

Color Correction

What PowerPoint offers:

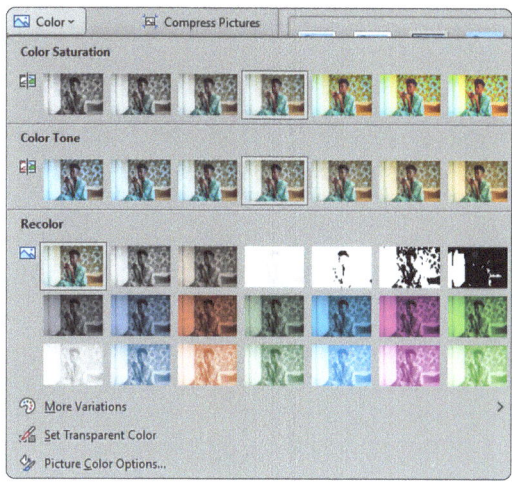
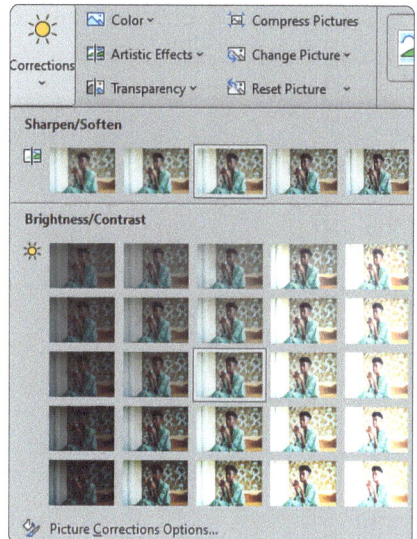

Some things will be found under **Picture Format Ribbon > Color**, some will be found under **Picture Format Ribbon > Corrections**. Let's review.

Color menu

Saturation
There are 7 presets for saturation. You can try to get finer control if you use the Format Picture pane instead. (Right click the image and choose "Format Picture.")

Tone
What I typed for Saturation goes here, too. I don't wanna retype it and you don't want to re-read it.

Recolor
This one gives you 21 presets right off the bat. Yee. Haw.

The top row is just some standard sepia, black and white stuff. The rest of it? It pulls from the theme colors to make monotone images.

Set Transparent Color
Sort of but not quite the same as the Remove Background tool. It's good if you want to set **one VERY specific color**. Remove Background (which we'll talk about shortly) basically lets you set many colors as transparent.

Corrections

Sharpen/Soften
You get 5 options on the spectrum of Sharpen to Soften. Meh. I never use it.

Brightness/Contrast
THIS one gives you 25 presets. And many of them look the same to me.

And don't forget: You can try to get finer control if you use the Format Picture pane instead. (Right click the image and choose "Format Picture.")

Filters

What PowerPoint offers:

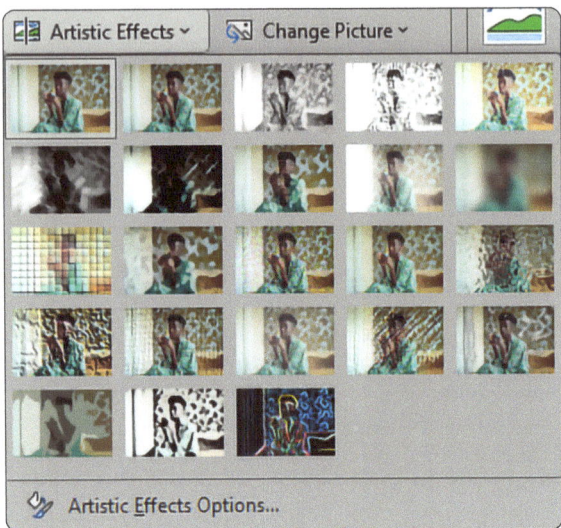

You know what? I've ignored these "artistic" effects my whole career. Because, really, this is PowerPoint. It can't do cool photo filter stuff.

For the most part, I still don't like the filters. BUT! There ARE a couple that I kinda love. (I know, I'm shocked, too.)

I've put examples of all of the preset effects below. I LOVE the sketch effects. And if I were to tell the truth, I think PowerPoint does a WAY better job than Photoshop!

Row 1:   Marker, Pencil Grayscale, Pencil Sketch, Line Drawing, Chalk Sketch
Row 2:   Paint Strokes, Paint Brush, Glow Diffuse, Blur, Light Screen
Row 3:   Watercolor Sponge, Film Grain, Mosaic Bubbles, Glass, Cement
Row 4:   Texturizer, Criss Cross Etching, Pastels Smooth, Plastic Wrap, Cut Out
Row 5:   Photocopy, Glowing Edges

Styles

What PowerPoint offers:

Styles include all of the things on the left, and again PowerPoint offers a lot of presets. And again...I never use these because I've not had a use case for them. However, I encourage you to play around with them.

Removing Backgrounds

What PowerPoint offers:

Original Image   Using the Tool   Result

Earlier I told you how you can set one single transparent color. With the **Remove Background** tool, you can get rid of a range of color by drawing a line across the colors you don't want.

So see? You have options! You might not have to use Photoshop. Between you, me, and these pages, I'll always use Photoshop for this. Don't tell anyone.

Transparency

What PowerPoint offers:

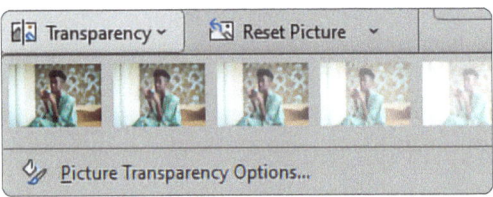

You know, for a LONG time we couldn't make pictures transparent at all. Like, it wasn't added to 365 until 2021!

If you have a stand alone version from before 2021, you also won't have it. (Apparently even to this day.) If you're one of the unlucky ones who doesn't have this function, there's a workaround!

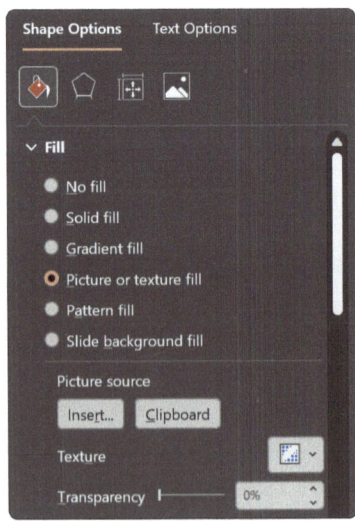

And the workaround is....
1. Draw a shape
2. Fill with the picture you want to use
3. Adjust the shape's transparency

3D

You may be used to:

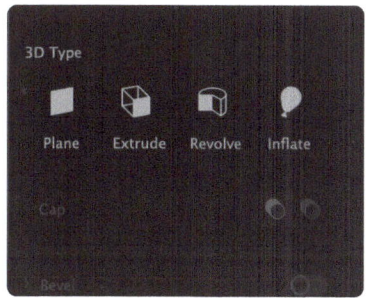

What PowerPoint offers:

You probably think of these tools when you think of 3D anything in PowerPoint. And yes, these tools are all still there. I never bothered using them, even when we were in the throws of Y2K design.

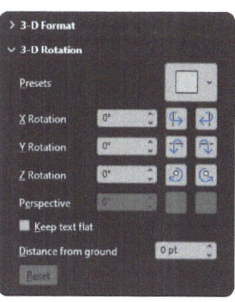 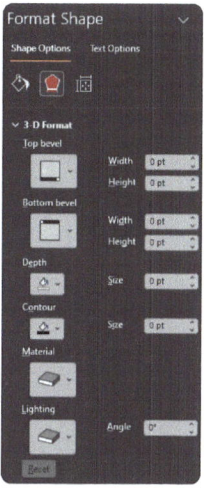  

What's SUPER cool is that there's some really amazing 3D models that you can add to your slides now. And you can animate them so that they can show different points of view of those models. Head to the **Insert Ribbon** to play around.

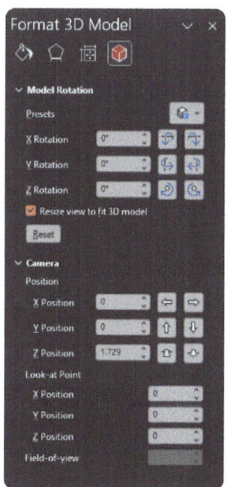 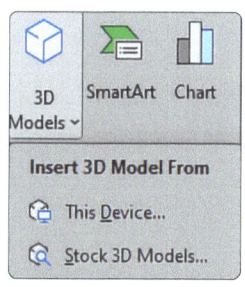 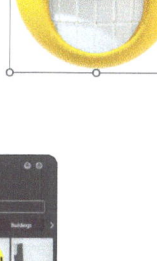

63

Tables: don't make fake ones. Please.

Seriously. Do you know how many times I have seen people build tables out of rectangles, lines, and text boxes? WAY TOO MANY. More often than not, I see that in Creative Suite projects. So let's just all agree right now that we're going to use the table tool as it's intended.

PowerPoint Location

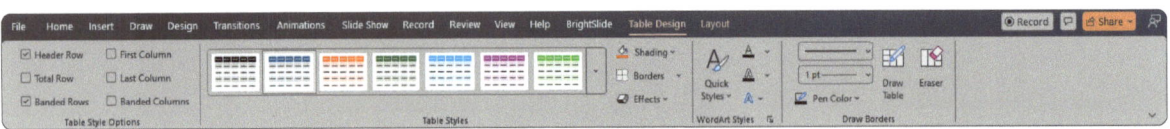

Select your table, then: **Table Design Ribbon**

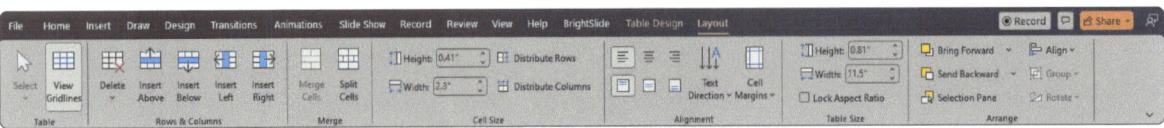

Select your table, then: **Layout Ribbon**

Insert Table

You may be used to:

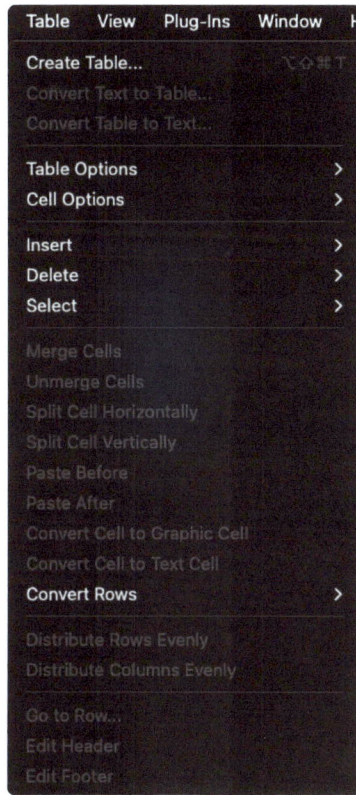

What PowerPoint offers:

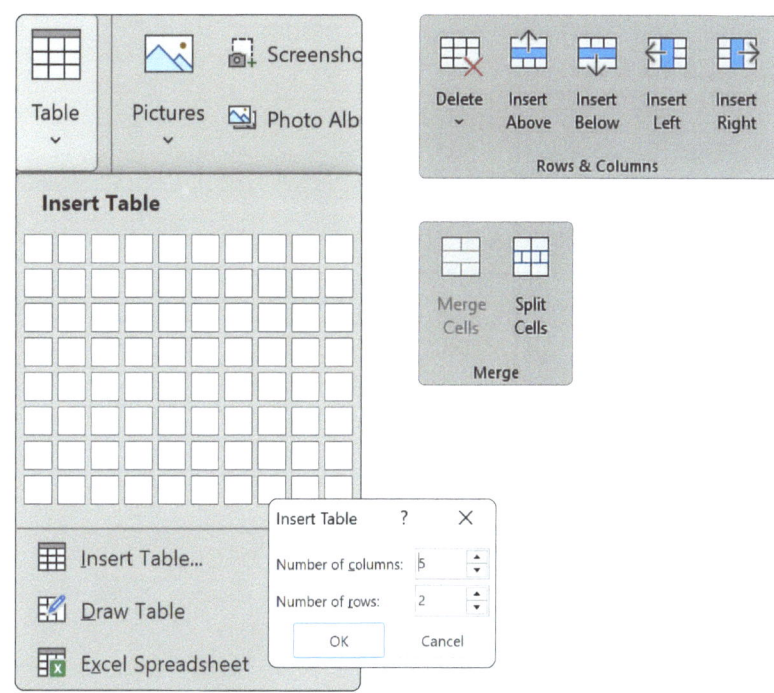

Go to **Insert Ribbon > Table**. I know what the first thing is that you'll say: "But I need a table that's bigger than THAT." It's OK. You can either start with a smaller one and add rows and columns or just choose "Insert Table..." to be specific.

Table Styles

You may be used to:

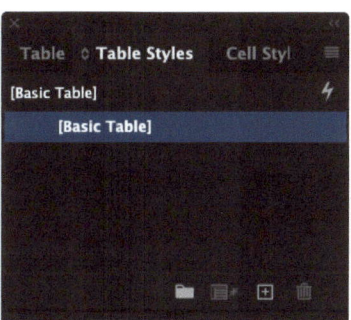

What PowerPoint offers:

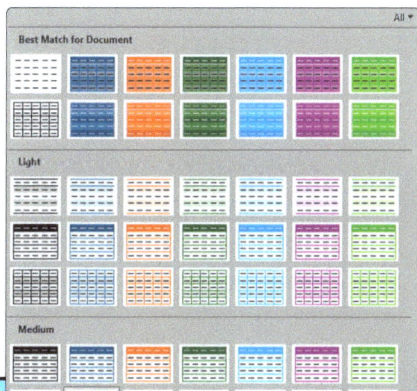

PowerPoint give you a bunch of preset styles, but they're all ugly.

Not only that, you can't save a custom table style! So your best bet is to style one table the way you like it, copy/paste it, and then edit the contents.

65

Table Elements

You may be used to:

Table options in InDesign.

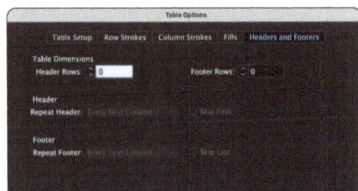

What PowerPoint offers:

Select table > Table Design ribbon

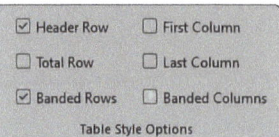

Use these. Use these and THEN style your table. OK, at least ALWAYS use the Header Row because you need it programmatically added in for **screen readers** to do their job properly.

Border Formatting

You may be used to:

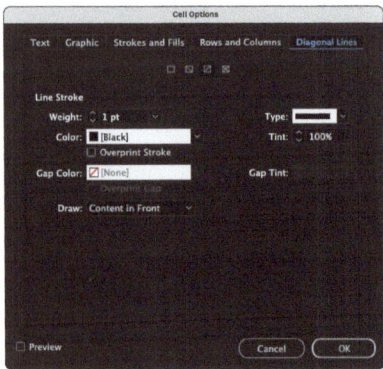

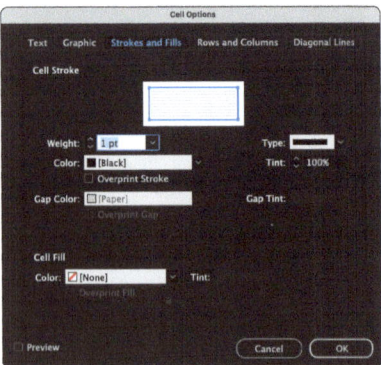

What PowerPoint offers:

Dare I say, PowerPoint can do everything InDesign can do when it comes to borders. Even diagonal lines! (Honestly, I'm just now learning that.)

How you COLOR the borders, however, it a bit clunky. The order of operations is:

1. Pen color
2. Line type/thickness
3. **THEN** the borders you want to apply all that to.

Cell Formatting

You may be used to:

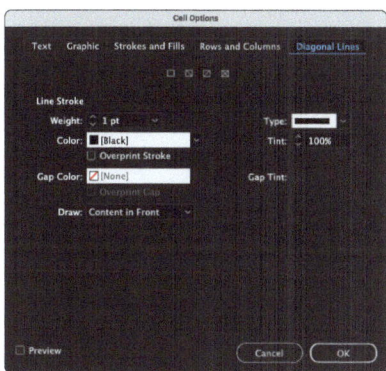

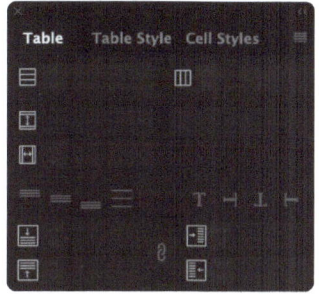

What PowerPoint offers:

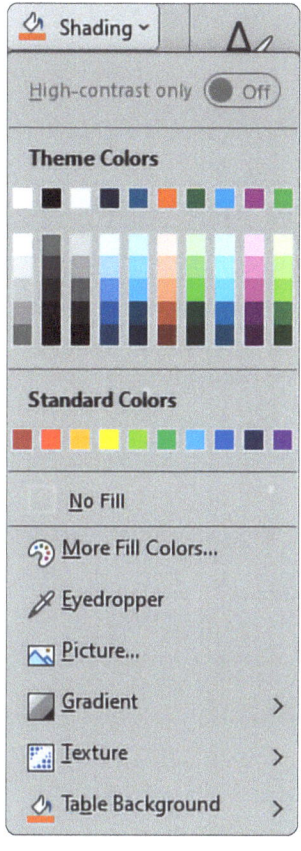

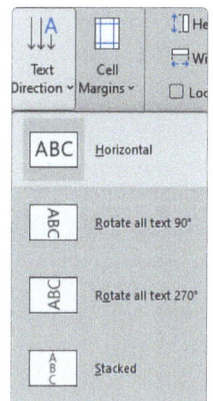

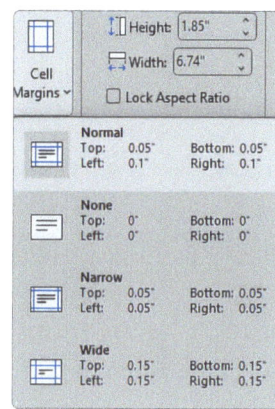

I have good news and bad news. You can't put images in cells. (This is something I really wish I could do in Excel, but that's a whole other can of worms.)

BUT! You CAN decimal-align numbers! It's VERY not easy to spot. In fact, the thing you have to click on is so small, I don't know if my screenshot will be high enough resolution for print. Forgive me if this is blurry.

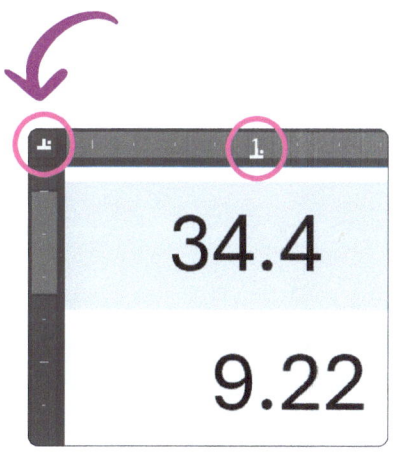

Select your numbers, click on the tiny button at the corner of the rulers until you get 🝱, and then click on the ruler where you want the tab stop to be. You have to have a TAB character before the number (CTRL + TAB). Or go to **More Paragraph Options** (nubbin in that part of the ribbon), then choose TABS... and set them.

Columns and bars and pie, oh my!

I can confidently say right here that you don't have any good charting solutions in Adobe's Creative Suite. Sure, you can make a chart in Illustrator, but it's horrible. It's got the same level of usability now as it did decades ago.

Go to **Insert Ribbon > Chart**. When you do, you'll get this popup with a bunch of choices.

After you choose one, a small spreadsheet will pop up where your data goes. It's an embedded spreadsheet, not a separate file, and should stay that way or you're going to have tons of problems updating the chart in the future.

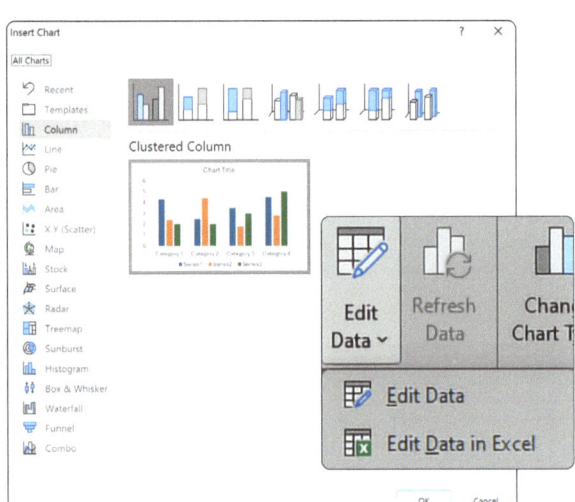

PowerPoint Location

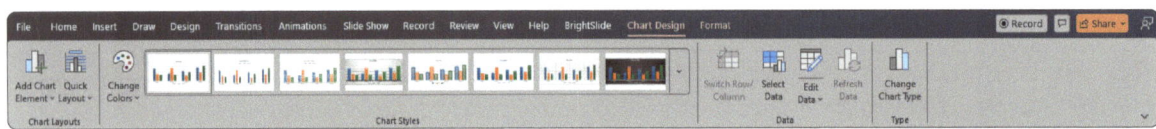

Select your chart, then: **Chart Design Ribbon**

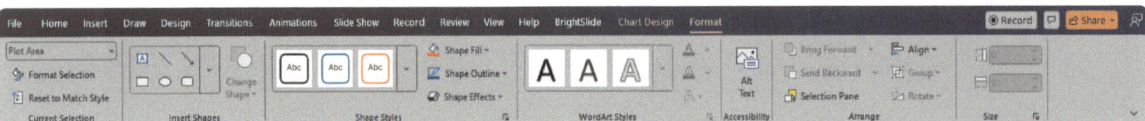

Select your chart, then: **Format Ribbon**

Types of Charts

Look at all of the glorious options you get in PowerPoint!!! **Amazeballs.** If you want to know when to use each kind of chart, I'll put some cool things in the resources section at the end.

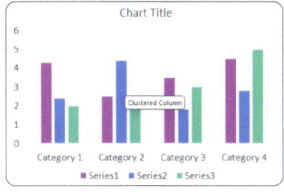
Column

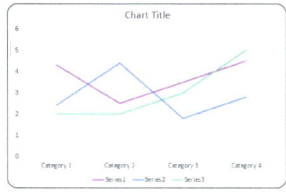
Line

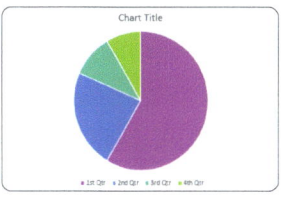
Pie

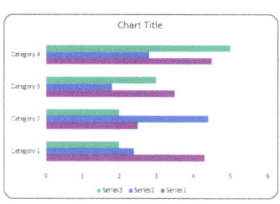
Bar

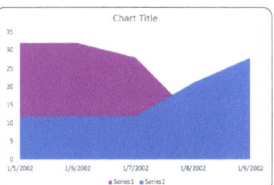
Area

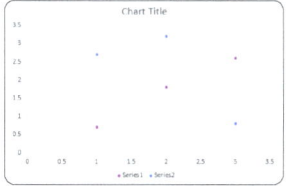
Scatter Plot

Map

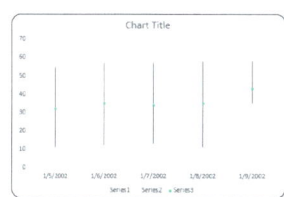
Stock

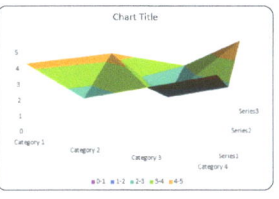
Surface

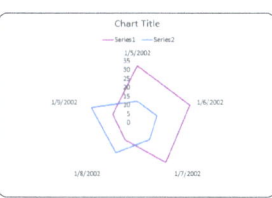
Radar

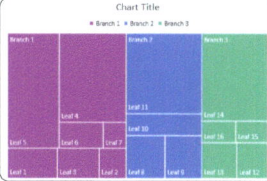
Treemap

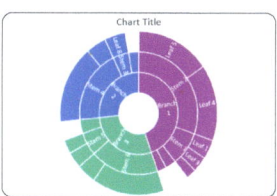
Sunburst

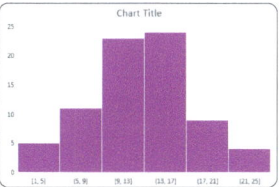
Histogram

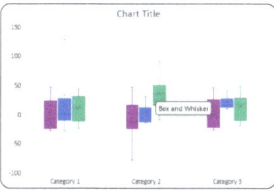
Box & Whisker

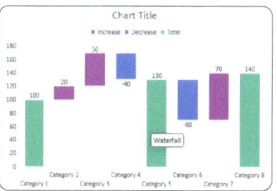
Waterfall

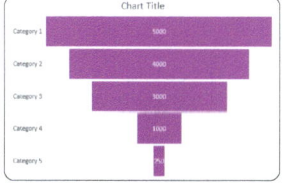
Funnel

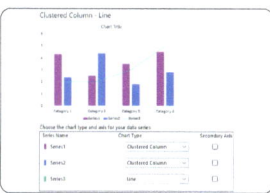
Combo

Adding Chart Elements

First up in the **Chart Design Ribbon** is your go-to place for adding chart elements. You're not going to get this kind of control in Illustrator. Here's a quick guide.

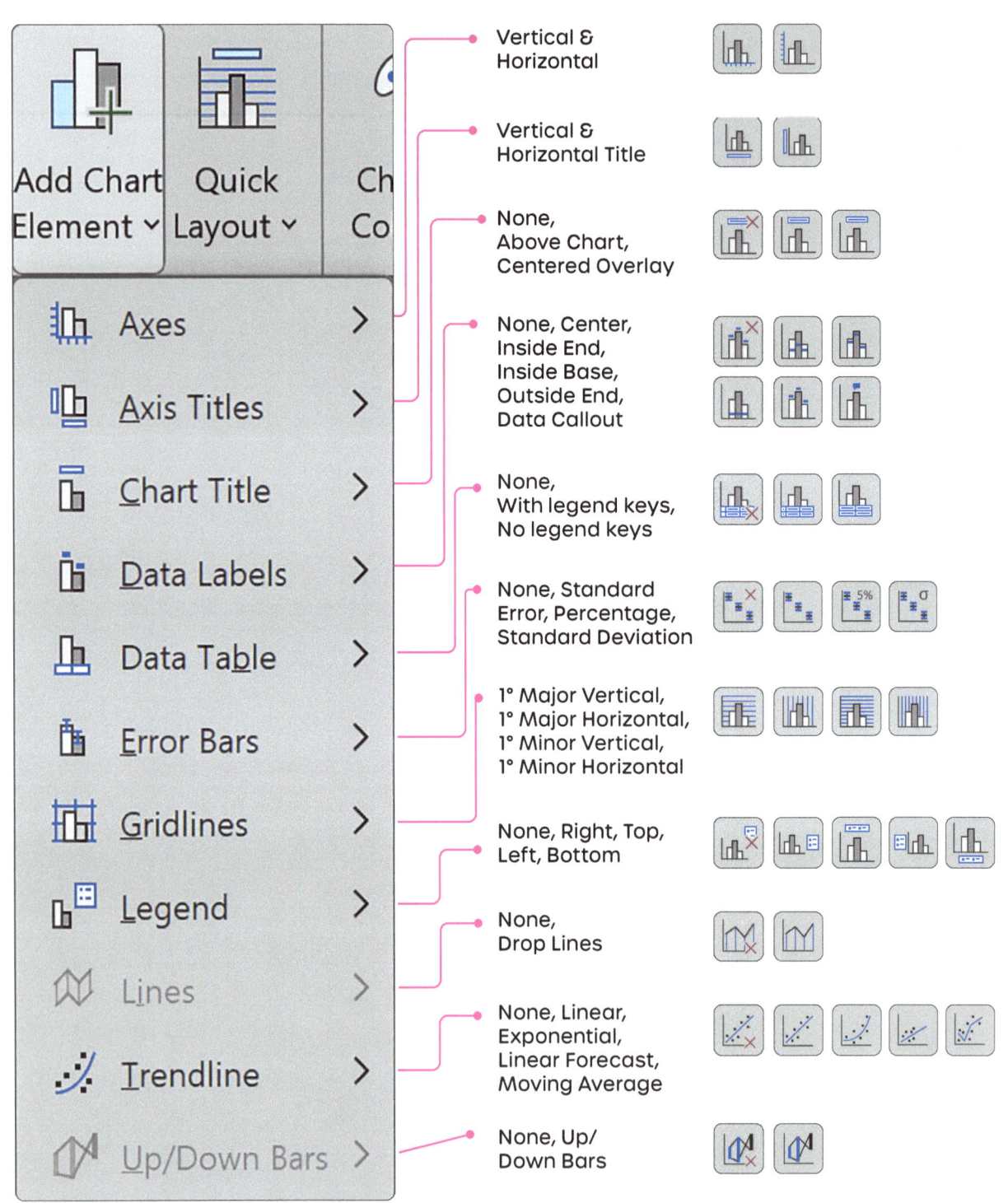

Quick Layouts & Colors

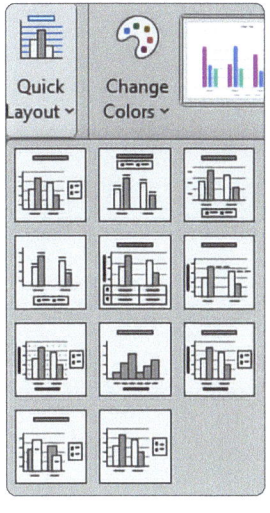
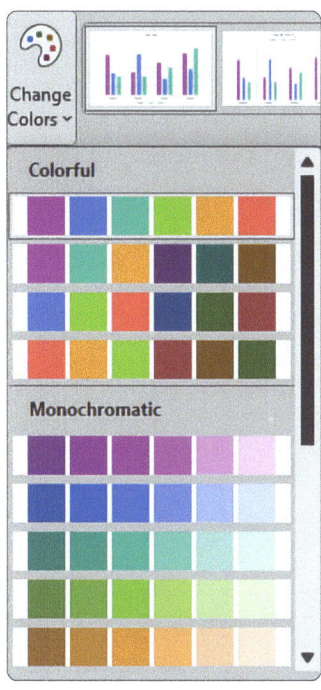

If you're not sure what you want displayed in your chart apart from data, you can always noodle around with Quick Layouts.

My recommendation? It's a good start. Don't end there. Take away chart junk until you get to the point where the next thing you take away renders the chart useless. Then put that one thing back.

There are also color sets you can pick from for your chart colors. By default, your chart colors pull from your current theme. I don't recommend using these monochromatic options. They'll create accessibility issues.

Formatting Axes

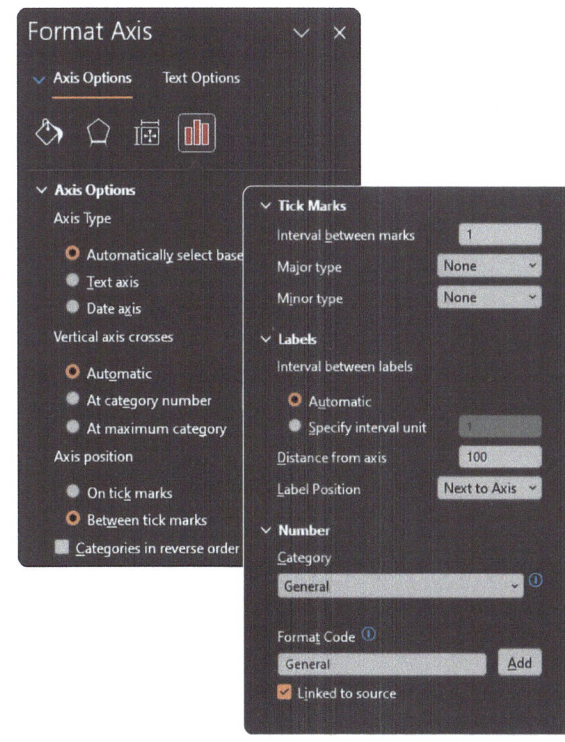

See how much GLORIOUS control we have over charts in PowerPoint? (You're tired of me saying shit like this, aren't you?) Why would you even dream of doing this in Illustrator?

You have visual control over major and minor tick marks, where they sit, axis labels. You can set what type of data the X axis is displaying (under Axis Options). You can set where the Y axis crosses the X axis.

And you can specify the format of your numbers. Just be careful with percentages. If you show 70% in the chart when the data in the spreadsheet is 70 instead of 0.7, you'll get 7000% here.

Formatting Series & Data Points

You can change the appearance of an entire series or a single data point. Just double-click until you have what you want selected, right-click, and choose **Format Data Series**.

There are 3 sets of things you can change: Fill, Effects, and Series Options.

For the love of all that is good in this world, please never put effects on your data. Or your chart. Just. Don't.

You can format the legend, as well. Select it, right-click on it, and choose **Format Legend**.

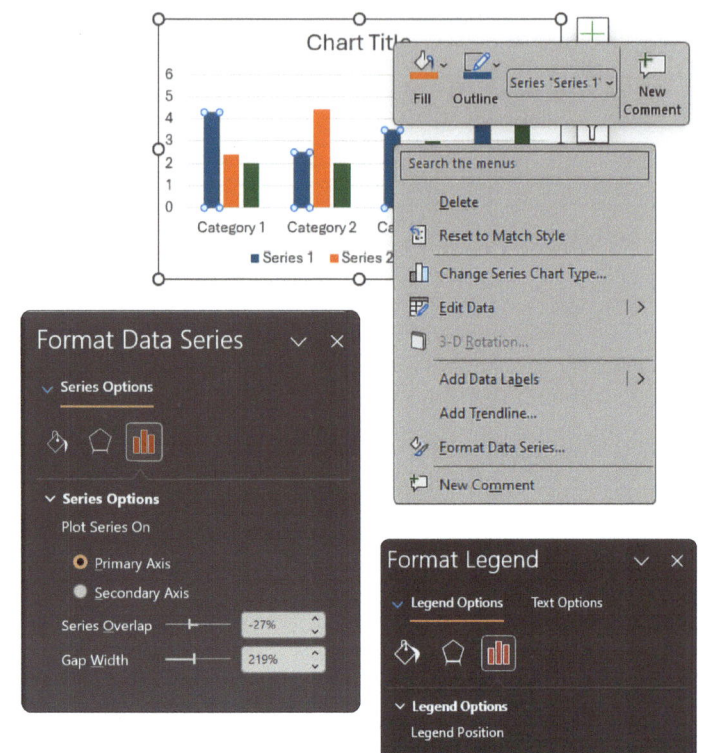

Data Tables

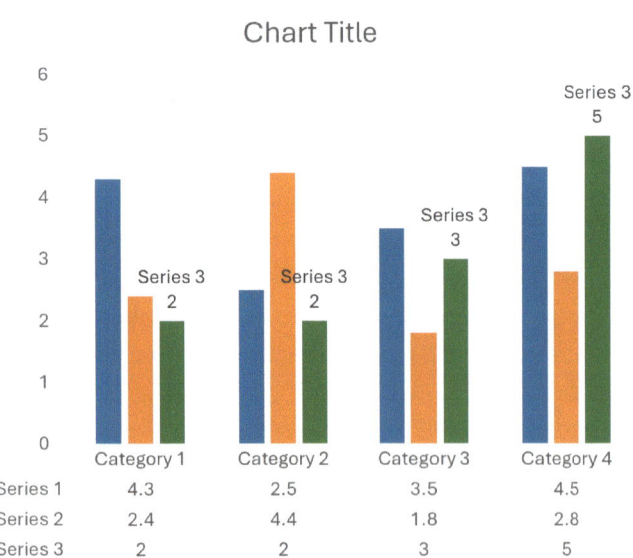

I have mixed feelings about data tables. One one hand, it's a great idea, accessibility-wise. On the other hand, you don't have a lot of control over its appearance or HOW FREAKING CLOSE that table is to the X axis.

LOOK AT IT.

And you only SOME have control over the borders.

72

Formatting Data Labels

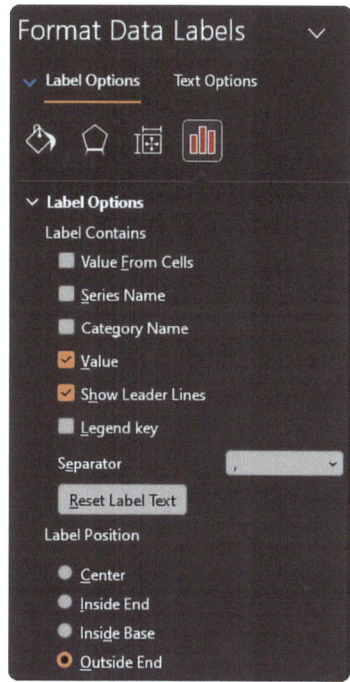

Have I said how much I like the amount of control we have over charts in PowerPoint? I have?

Data labels have a ton of options. My favorite settings are:

- Category Name
- Value
- No leader lines
- Separator is (New Line)

Just remember: don't add too much stuff to your charts. People need to understand what the chart is about without having to think too much.

Formatting Numbers

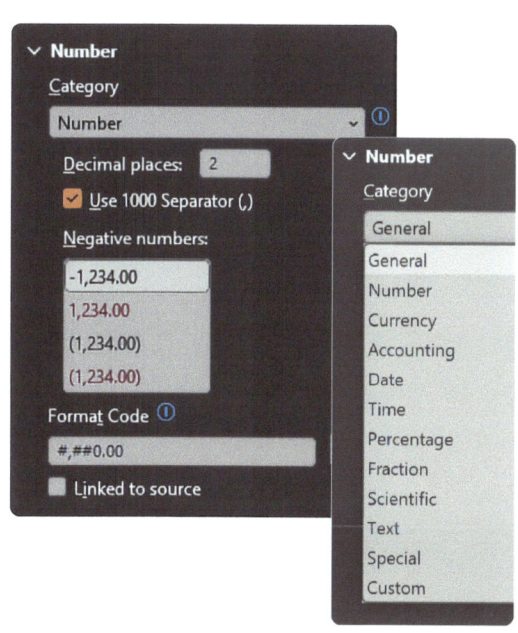

OK. Numbers. I touched on them two pages ago. Let's go a little deeper. You've got a lot of number categories to choose from and they each have their own subset of settings.

By far, the most interesting one is the **Custom** setting. You can type in a special formula and makes some pretty cool things happen.

You might also find that you'll be on Google a lot searching for ways to fix what you typed in.

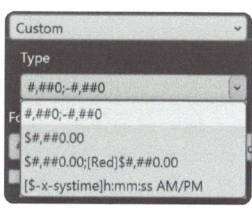

Video (and audio)

So, you've decided to spice up your PowerPoint with some video. Good choice—because nothing says, "I'm serious about this presentation," like a well-placed clip. PowerPoint does a decent job here, but there are a few gotchas that might frustrate you a bit.

Don't expect the finesse of Premiere Pro—you won't be editing the next Sundance hit—but for embedding videos, trimming them, and even adding some basic effects, PowerPoint does the trick.

You may be used to:

PowerPoint Location

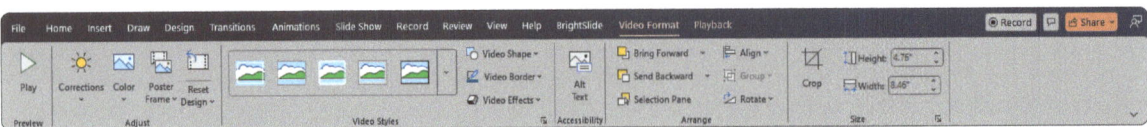

Select your video, then: **Video Format Ribbon**

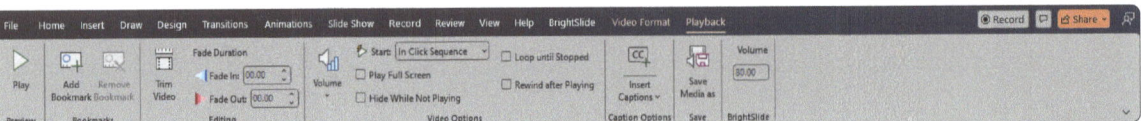

Select your video, then: **Playback Ribbon**

Inserting Video & Audio

First up? Video.

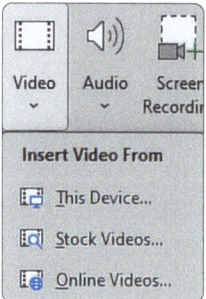

Found in the **Insert Ribbon**.

Stock Video

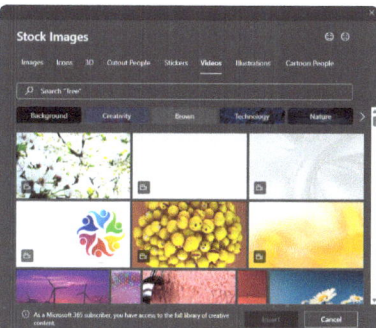

You know? I never honestly thought this would happen—stock video that I don't have to pay extra for. And there's some pretty decent videos to choose from.

Online Video

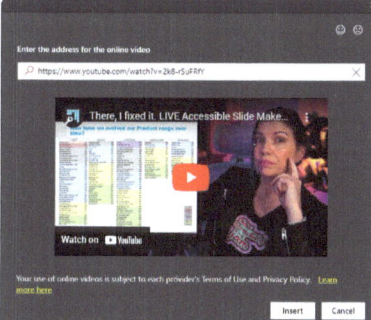

When the link is valid, you'll see a preview here.

Supported video providers:
- YouTube
- SlideShare
- Vimeo
- Stream
- Flip

But be careful which URL you paste in. Read on.

Since YouTube seems to be the most common, it's worth noting that you have to use the browser URL.

Don't use the YouTube share link. It won't work.

Adding Audio

Do you see it? There's an inconsistency in the UI! (Compared to the Insert Video button.) And bummer, no stock audio. (That was written sarcastically. We don't need to be putting audio in all willy-nilly.)

Screen Recordings

If you can't seem to remember how to make screen recordings, PowerPoint makes it easy. They give you a whole built in tool!

75

Video Format

Format Pane

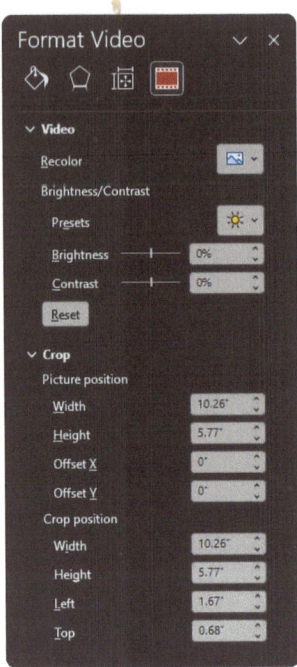

You've got some pretty basic stuff here. You get two color correction options to play with: recoloring and brightness/contrast.

And you can crop your videos.

If you find that you need to trim some stuff off of your video, you don't need another piece of software to do it. This brings me joy.

Trimming Video

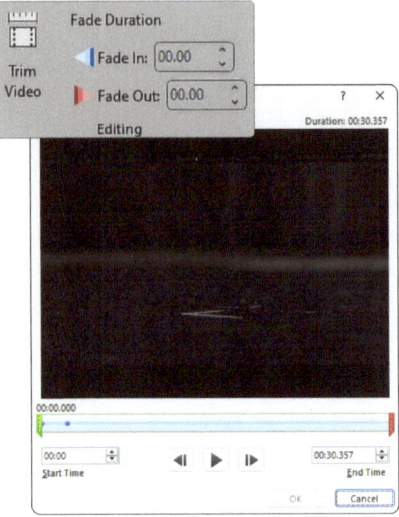

Poster Frames

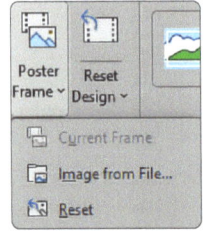

When you don't like the preview photo of the video that sits on the slide after you put it there, great news! You can add your own poster frame. Just make sure it's a 16:9 ratio.

Video Playback

Captions

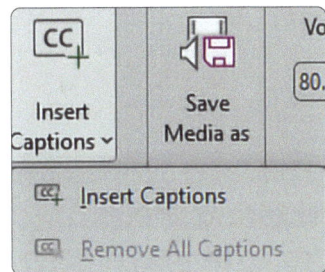

This one kills me. Yes! We can insert our own caption file! But it's a WebVTT file. Which means you need some other software to make it. If you put an online video in, you'll be OK since the tools in the YouTube player carry into PowerPoint..

Set When Video Starts

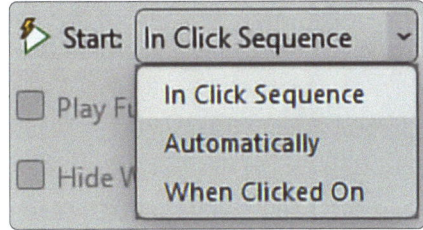

And don't forget to think about when you want the video to play? By default, it's set to "In Click Sequence," but you have these other options to choose from.

Bookmarks

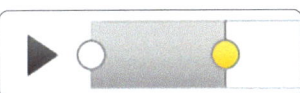

Did you know you can add bookmarks to video? You might be wondering why you would want to do that. Well...

Bookmarks & Triggers

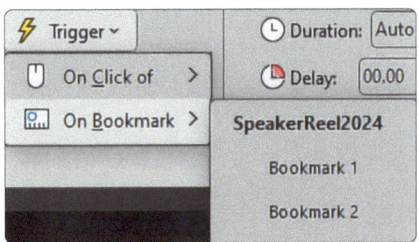

...because if you have some cool animation happening on your slide, you might want certain parts of the animation to start playing at a specific point in the video. You use bookmarks as triggers for those things to happen.

'Tis pretty handy except that you can't rename bookmarks.

Animation...more capable than you think.

Animations in PowerPoint are surprisingly robust, considering the program's primary purpose isn't to replace After Effects. (But you COULD for some projects.) This section is going to be hard to write because, well, these pages are static. Don't worry, I'll show you cool stuff in the videos.

Types of Animation

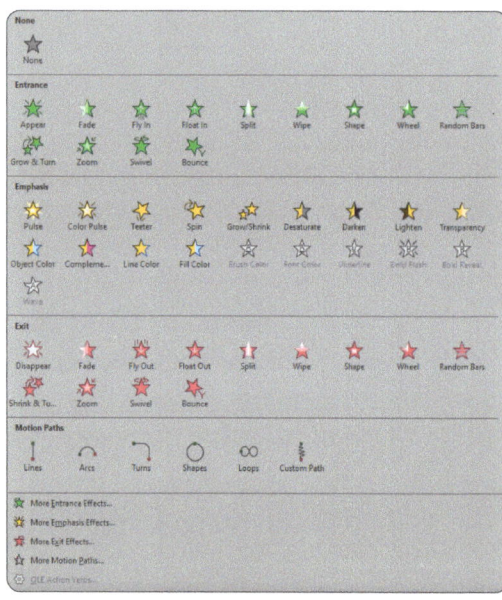

When you insert an animation, you have 4 categories to choose from:
- Entrance effects
- Emphasis effects
- Exit effects
- Motion paths

You can put several animations on an object and create some spectacular things.

A tip for Mac users: if you want to add more than one animation to an object, you can't have any animations in the animation pane selected. If you do, you'll just replace the animation you just added.

PowerPoint Location

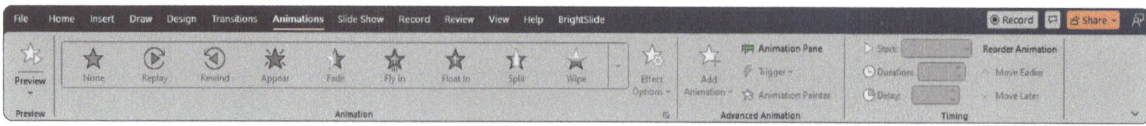

Select your object and go to the **Animation Ribbon**.

Timing & Effects

The Basics

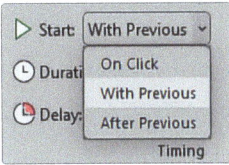 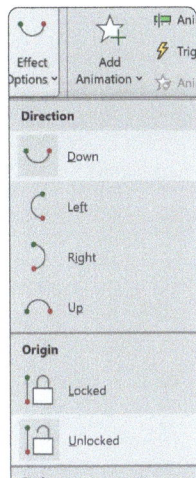

You might be familiar with these...SO basic.

You can set an animation to start either:
- On Click
- With Previous
- After Previous

You can set how long it should take to complete that animation and you can delay it.

Each animation has its own set of effects, too. Make sure you check out the options each animation offers.

The Cool Shit

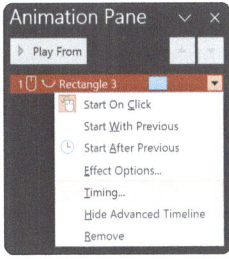

There's cooler stuff you can do, but there's no button in the ribbon for advanced timing options. You have to go to the animation pane to see the dropdown.

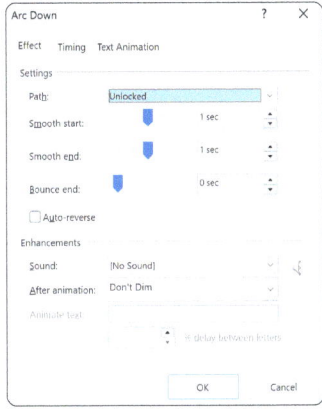 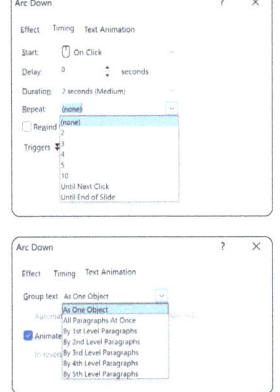

One of the things you definitely should be using is the Timing tab in the big modal that pops up. **This is where you'll find easing.**

(PowerPoint just calls it "Settings.")

You'll also find options to repeat, reverse, and do fancy things with text.

Triggers

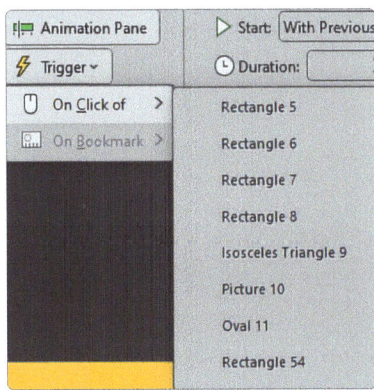

Think of these as dependent actions. If you want Animation 1 to be dependent on Action 3, this is how we do it. (Now that song is stuck in my head.)

If you do start using triggers a lot, do yourself a favor and rename everything in the selection pane in a descriptive way so you can easily find your target object..

Animation Timeline

You probably won't like this.

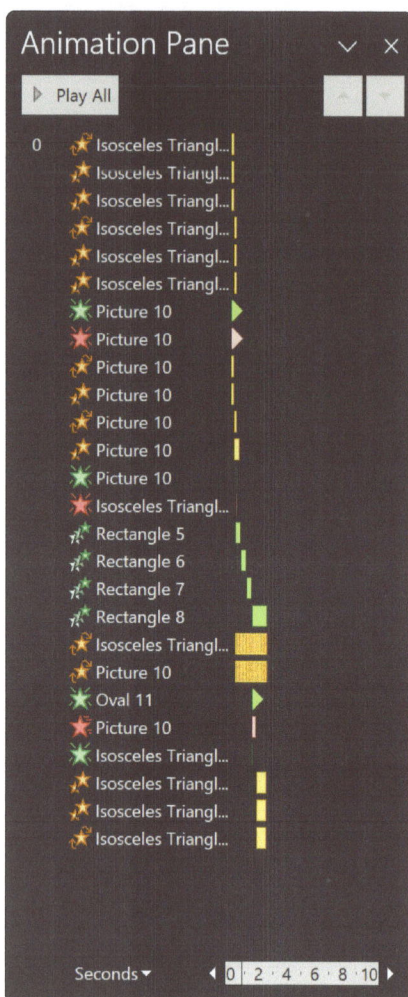

First off, you can find this in the **Animation Ribbon**. It's a smaller button labeled "Animation Pane." Surprising, I know.

Let's talk about the timeline you get to work with in PowerPoint, you lucky duck, you.

It sucks.

It's not like anything you're used to. It's hard to fine tune things in there and you can easily screw things up if you're not careful.

All of the panes are docked on the right by default. BUT! **Did you know that panes don't have to be docked at all?** That's right!

When you really start getting into animation, I highly recommend you drag the animation pane to a second monitor and make it full screen. It doesn't make the animation pane less finicky, but at least you'll be able to zoom in and see details a little better.

Animation Pane

Docked Pane

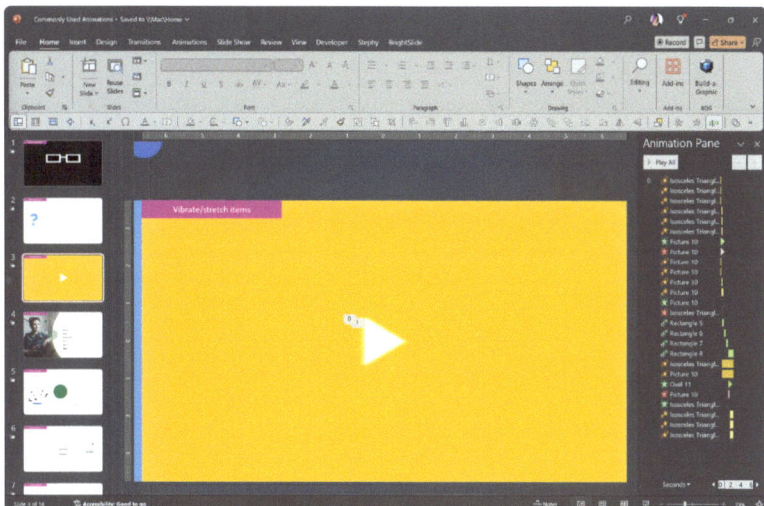

Just grab the top of the pane with your mouse, drag, and POOF! You can put that anywhere.

To re-dock a pane, just drag it to the side where it was, just like you would in InDesign or Photoshop or whatever.

Undocked Pane

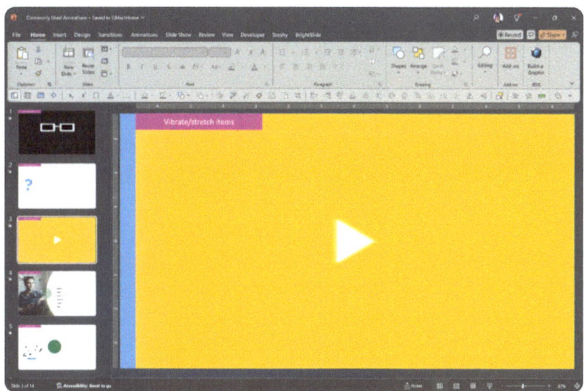

~~Thing~~ Screen 1

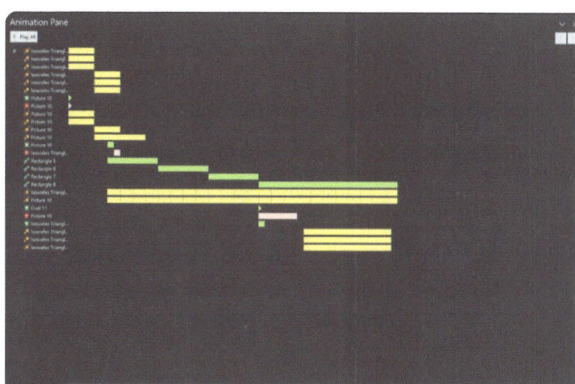

~~Thing~~ Screen 2

Transitions

Animations are contained on one slide. Transitions go across slides and you have a lot of choices. That doesn't mean you should take advantage of most of them. (Although, I can't begrudge anyone a decent Glitter transition.)

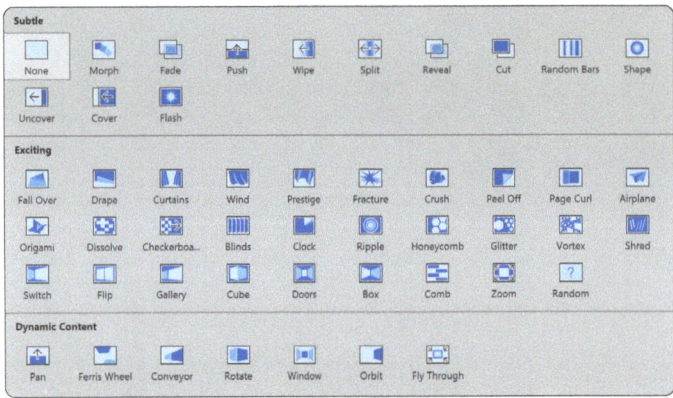

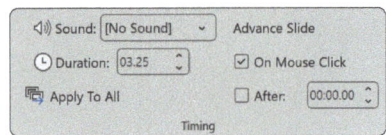

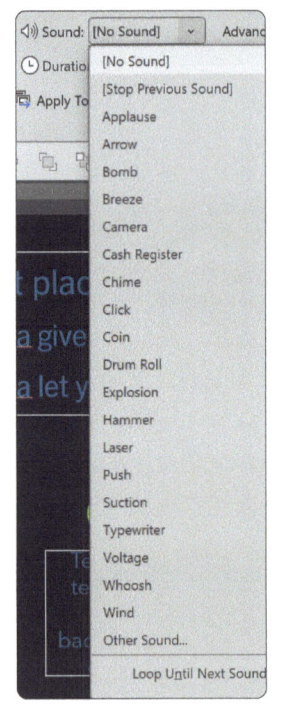

Look how many there are! Go ahead and play with them. But I humbly ask that you stick with None, Morph, and Fade.

Yes, there will be some very niche circumstances where the other transitions might work well. For the most part, stick with the first 3.

Morph is my favorite. If you've ever used Keynote, this is the equivalent to Magic Move. Duplicate one of your slides and on the second one, change the position, shape, and color of some of the things on it. Apply Morph to the **second slide** and watch the magic happen.

These are generally silly. Please avoid using them unless you have a REALLY good reason to.

If you really need origami cranes in your life, go ahead and tear this page out and make one.

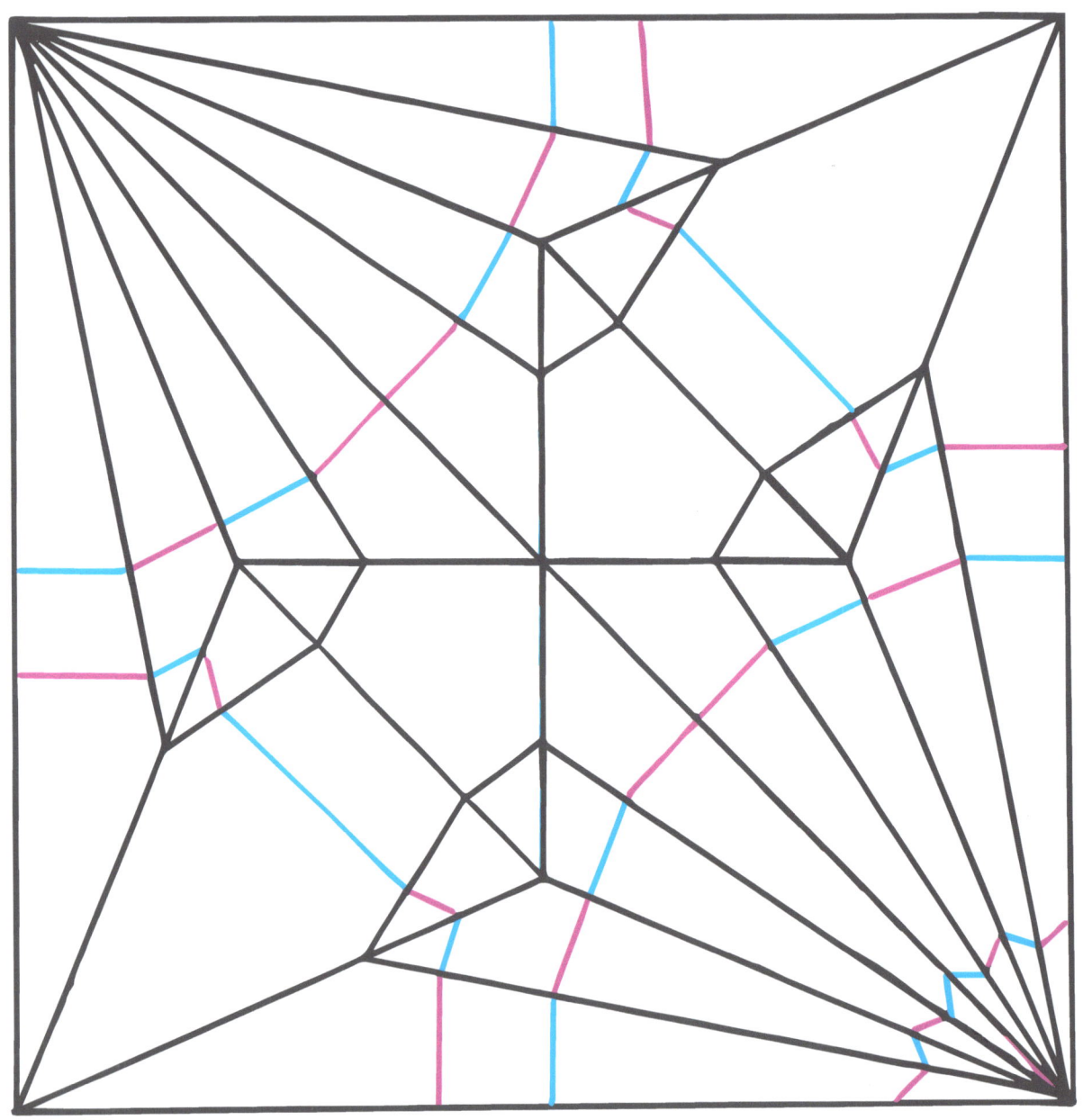

Let's talk accessible presentations.

Before I get on my soapbox, let's talk about the word itself. Accessibility is long word (although not as long as "presentations"—I mean LOOK at it). It's annoying to type out and it just takes up a LOT of room on the page. (Like this rant.) So I'll use the abbreviation "a11y" when I remember to. Just wanted to let you know. (That's an eleven in there, not 2 Ls, which is how many letters there are in the word.)

Our goal here is to make the presentation experience equally awesome for everyone. Please make sure your decks are accessible.

Don't panic.

It's not that hard to do.

The Accessibility Checker: Mostly Reliable

Yes, that's right. It's not 100% accurate. Please see page 108 for all of the ways you'll need to check manually.

PowerPoint Location

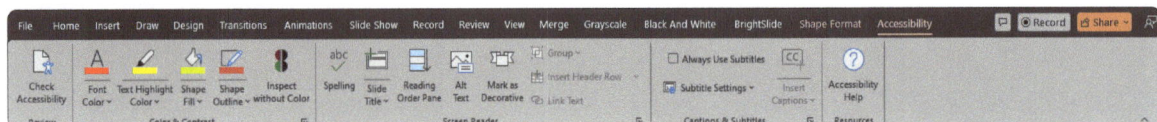

Review Ribbon > Check Accessibility

PowerPoint has a built-in tool that helps you track accessibility issues as you're creating your presentation. It works like live preflight in InDesign and it's checking for:

- Alt text in
    - Pictures
    - SmartArt
    - Graphics
    - Shapes
    - Groups
    - Charts
    - Embedded objects
    - Ink
    - Video
- Slide content is read by a screen reader in the order you intend
- The color contrast between text and background colors is high enough
- Every slide has a unique title (sometimes this is intentional and there's a workaround to maintain accessibility–see tip on right.)
- Table structure is simple and uses table headers

But when we're talking about making sure something you create is accessible, no quick checker or automated tool is going to catch everything, nor is it going to suggest ways to elegantly design a fix.

Make use of the a11y checker because it'll help you fix things. If you click on one of the results in the a11y pane, PowerPoint shows you **Additional Information** below telling you:
- Why it needs to be fixed
- How to fix it

Not only that, PowerPoint will automatically take you to the slide the issue is on AND select the object in question.

AND NOW!!! Get this...

You can click on the down arrow next to the issue in the pane and it'll give you options to choose from that, when selected, **PERFORMS THE FIX FOR YOU**.

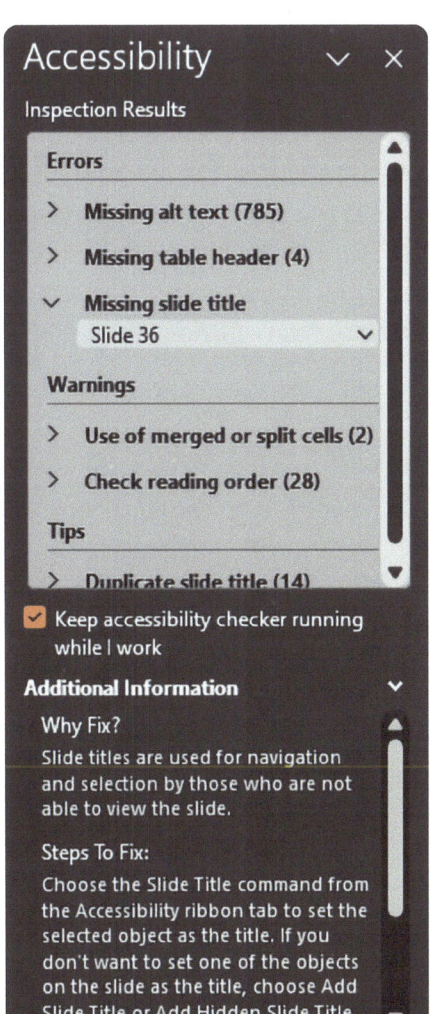

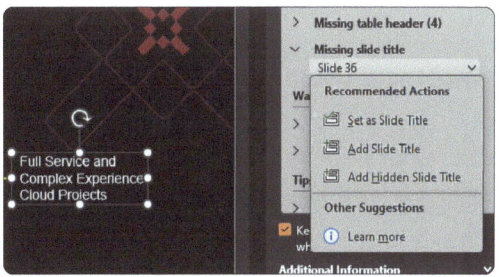

Some A11y Design Basics

I'm not going to go into detail about accessible design in this book. That should be a whole other book entirely because there's so much. (Hey, that's a great idea, Steph! Maybe next year.)

Color

Let's start with color. First thing we need to remember is that **color can't be used as the only indicator of meaning**.

When you're presenting a large, nicely designed statistic and want to indicate that a number is bad, you can't just use red. Instead, try adding a down arrow or even a sad face.

When adding links into a slide, make sure they're not just a different color, **add an underline to your link formatting**. (And while we're talking about underlines, only ever use underlines for links. It's a design pattern that is so ingrained into people's brains, that they'll think your emphasis underline is actually a link. And they'll try to interact with it.)

Creating Accessible Color Themes

These tips will help you whether you're assessing an existing color theme or creating your own.

But first, let's review how color themes work. In PPT, you can program in a total of 12 colors into a theme—4 total dark and light colors, and text colors, 6 accent colors, and two link colors (active and visited).

The dark and light colors are default background and text colors. The accent colors in the top row are the colors that determine the colors of carts, tables, and smart art in the order in which the color chips appear. So it's important that these accents, when directly next to each other, are distinguishable from its neighbor.

Text

How text is treated can really affect the understanding of the content by those with cognitive-, sight-, and even hearing-related impairments.

First, make sure your text is legible and readable. Legibility is the appearance of fonts or text.

Readability is a measure of how difficult a paragraph is to read and understand.

Legibility of your content in PowerPoint can be controlled in a few different ways.

Pick a safe font. Not all fonts work in PowerPoint everywhere. Safe fonts play nicely across all operating systems and versions of PPT. If a font isn't present on another Machine, font substitution will occur and can look something like this:

As for readable text, make sure you're **using simple language**. Avoid too many acronyms or corporate speak.

- Avoid too many acronyms
- Use simple language instead of corporate speak
- Use whitespace wisely.

Format your content in a way that eases our audience's cognitive load by way of a **good use of white space**.

- Font-size
- Kerning
- Line-height
- Line length
- Column gutters
- Cell padding
- Tab stops
- Indents

And always remember that **if everything is important, nothing is**. If you look at a slide and thing that it's just. Too. Much. Think of those living with ADHD who are trying to understand what your takeaways are.

You might also be picking up on the fact that many fixes to accessibility issues are also just best design practices.

Alt Text

Anything that is visual, that isn't live text, and that conveys meaningful information needs to have alt text. If an icon, shape, or other visual piece isn't conveying important information, you can mark them as decorative.

How to add Alt Text:

- Right-click on the object
- Choose "edit alt text"
- Enter in descriptive alt text
- Or mark as decorative

Items that might need alt text:

- Images
- Icons
- Charts
- Tables
- Video
- Embedded objects

Examples of Good Alt Text

Okay: "Pancakes"
This alt text is only "okay" because it's not very descriptive. Yes, this is an image of a stack of pancakes. But, there's more to be said about this image.

Better: "Stack of buttermilk pancakes with a dab of butter and maple syrup."
This alt text is a better alternative because it is far more descriptive of what's in the image. This isn't just a stack of "pancakes" (as the first alt text example demonstrated); it's a stack of blueberry pancakes with a dusting of powdered sugar!

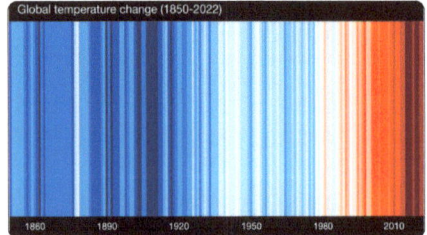

OK: "Climate stripes showing the change in global temperatures from 1850 to 2022."

Better: "Colored stripes of chronologically ordered temperatures where they increase in red to show the warming global temperature."

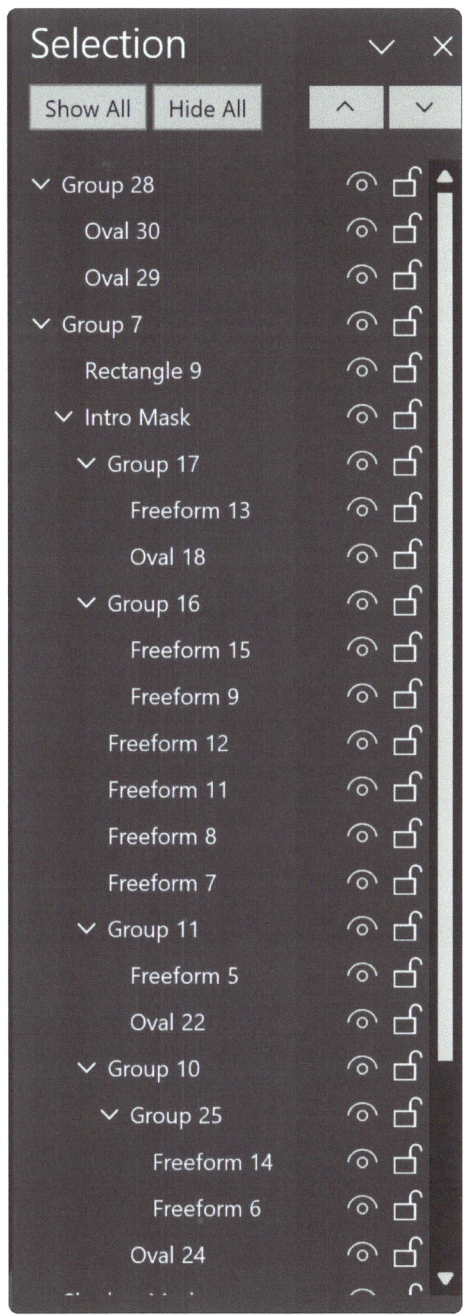

Screen Readers & Reading Order

There are two panes in PPT where you can adjust the tab or reading order of screen readers: the **reading order pane (PC only)** and the **selection pane**.

By default, a screen reader will read the slide title first, followed by other content in elements defined in the slide layout. Then it will read any additional content on the side in the order it was added to the slide.

Screen readers will read the content on your slides starting with the bottom layer and ending on the top in the **selection pane**.

It's the other way around in the Reading Pane. Why?

NO FREAKIN' CLUE.

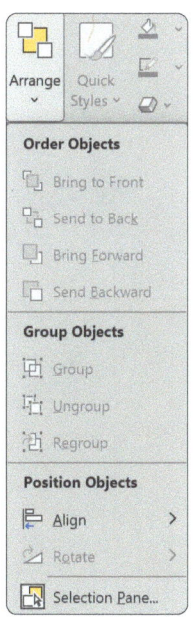

Accessing the Selection Pane

Home Tab > Arrange > Selection Pane

To reorder the objects on your slides, simply click and drag items in the selection pane (or reading pane).

Where is the reading order pane? It's in the accessibility ribbon.

The S.C.H.I.T. List

You read that correctly. Just like there's a difference between being **A** shit and being **THE** shit, the same is true for Shit Lists and the S.C.H.I.T. List. The official a11y guidelines (WCAG) uses POUR as an acronym for the 4 flavors of guidelines. Did I just throw that out the window and make up my own acronym? Hell yes I did. Pretty sure mine is more memorable.

Sight-related

Did you know that some people only see in grayscale? Wild, huh? In fact, that'll help us when we're checking our work later. What you and your presenters need to remember is that, while there will likely be at least one colorblind person in the audience, it's even more likely that many of those people experience other sight issues.

What you're designing for:

Permanent impairments:
- Blindness
- Low vision (e.g., tunnel vision, loss of peripheral vision)
- Color blindness
- Macular degeneration
- Retinal disorders
- Glaucoma or cataracts

Temporary impairments:
- Eye strain or fatigue
- Migraines affecting vision
- Post-operative vision issues
- Conjunctivitis or other infections

Situational impairments:
- Dim lighting or extreme brightness (screen glare)
- Small or distant screens
- Viewing through dirty or fogged glasses
- Reading in a moving vehicle

Design considerations:

WCAG 1.1.1, WCAG 1.3.2	Alt text for images, describe charts, use logical reading order
WCAG 1.3.1	Offer downloadable versions for custom display adjustments
WCAG 1.4.1	Avoid reliance on color alone to convey meaning
WCAG 1.4.3	Ensure high contrast between text, link text, and background
WCAG 1.4.3	Test for visibility in bright/dim environments
WCAG 1.4.4	Use larger fonts (16pt+), simple legible fonts
WCAG 1.4.4	Clear, easy-on-the-eyes fonts
WCAG 1.4.5	Avoid small visuals, provide summaries for text-heavy slides
WCAG 1.4.6	Avoid pure black on pure white & vice versa
WCAG 1.4.12	Avoid crowded slides, ensure clean layout with enough spacing
WCAG 2.3.1	Minimize animations and flashing elements

Cognition-related

Never the first thought, and sometimes the last, cognition-related issues always seem doomed to live in the garage with that long-forgotten about box that was "just to good to throw away." And yet, I would argue they are the most prolific.

What you're designing for:

Permanent impairments:
- ADHD
- Autism spectrum disorder
- Dyslexia
- Dyspraxia
- Dementia or Alzheimer's disease
- Traumatic brain injury (TBI) causing cognitive issues

Temporary impairments:
- Short-term memory loss
- Brain fog
- Burnout or mental fatigue
- Recovery from illness affecting mental clarity

Situational impairments:
- Multitasking or dividing attention
- High-stress situations (e.g., tight deadlines)
- Information overload
- Language barriers
- Reading in a moving vehicle

Design considerations:

WCAG 1.3.1	Structure content using headings, lists, and logical layouts
WCAG 2.4.3	Maintain a logical focus order for easy navigation
WCAG 2.4.6	Use descriptive slide titles and link text
WCAG 3.1.5	Ensure content is accessible for lower reading levels
WCAG 3.2.3	Ensure that navigation is consistent across slides or content areas
WCAG 3.3.2	Provide clear labels and instructions for any form elements or input fields
WCAG 1.4.8	Don't center large blocks of text.
WCAG 1.4.12	Give content room to breath with plenty of white space.

Hearing-related

Design-wise, you might not have to worry about this very much at all. In this day and age, you can embed a YouTube link and turn subtitles on. Done. You'll want to coach your speaker a bit, though.

What you're designing for:

Permanent impairments::
- Deafness
- Partial hearing loss
- Tinnitus
- Auditory processing disorder
- Cochlear implant users

Temporary impairments:
- Temporary hearing loss
- Sensitivity to sound after prolonged loud noise exposure

Situational impairments:
- Background noise
- Listening to presentations on mute (e.g., while commuting)
- Poor-quality audio on a device
- Inability to use headphones due to an environment

Design considerations:

WCAG 1.2.1	Provide transcripts for audio-only content
WCAG 1.2.2	Provide captions for prerecorded audio and video
WCAG 1.2.3	Provide audio descriptions or media alternatives for video
WCAG 1.2.4	Provide captions for live audio content (easy for online presenting)
WCAG 1.2.5	Ensure audio descriptions are included for important visual content
WCAG 1.4.2	Provide users control over auto-playing audio
WCAG 1.4.7	Ensure low or no background audio during spoken content

Interaction-related

Interaction

This one is for all of you who have to make interactive presentations that end up playing on kiosks. And for those of you who love to make games in PowerPoint as holiday cards for your friends. (Yes, people do that and they're amazing.)

What you're designing for:

Permanent impairments:
- Cerebral palsy
- Arthritis
- Tremors
- Muscular dystrophy
- Carpal tunnel syndrome

Temporary impairments:
- Broken bones or sprains
- Muscle strain
- Temporary nerve damage

Situational impairments:
- Working in gloves
- No keyboard or mouse
- Using a mobile device with one hand

Design considerations:

WCAG 2.1.1	Ensure all functionality is available via keyboard
WCAG 2.1.2	Ensure users can navigate out of interactive elements using the keyboard
WCAG 2.1.4	Provide character key shortcuts for easy navigation
WCAG 2.5.1	Ensure complex gestures have simpler alternatives
WCAG 2.5.2	Allow for the cancellation of accidental pointer actions
WCAG 2.5.4	Ensure all controls have labels and that actions are contextually clear
WCAG 2.5.5	Interactive elements should be at least 44px by 44px

Technology-related

Technology

Not only is this the last one in this list, it's also usually the last one people consider, if they consider it at all. Please consider it. Differences in software, hardware, and internet connection can really gum up all the hard work you've done.

What you're designing for:

Permanent impairments::
- Reliance on screen readers
- Need for voice recognition software
- Use of specialized keyboards or mouse alternatives

Temporary impairments:
- Hardware quality
- Software version
- Poor network or Wi-Fi connectivity

Situational impairments:
- Poor signal strength
- Limited data plans preventing video streaming
- Accessing content on older devices
- Working in "offline mode" due to internet outages

Design considerations:

WCAG 2.4.1	Provide mechanisms to bypass repetitive content (those multi-slide animations that use Morph or content builds)
WCAG 2.4.4	Ensure links are clear and meaningful even out of context
WCAG 2.4.10	Use safe fonts so that text looks consistent no matter the platform or software version
WCAG 4.1.3	Ensure compatibility with various input methods

Design for accessibility before & while you build.

Everyone loves a good checklist. I've made many over the years and lucky you, I'm putting them all in this book. I hope they're useful. Oh, and if you want to have the lists on single sheets of paper, use the QR code below to download pdfs.

Before you build.

Ideally, you'll write your content before you open your preferred slideware. Some of these things you might not do until you're actually building slides, especially if you haven't picked images and stuff yet.

WCAG 2.4.6 — Use plain language so people understand what you're saying faster. Put technical information in a handout.

WCAG 2.4.2 — Provide informative, unique slide titles.

WCAG 1.3.1 — Use headings to convey meaning and structure.

WCAG 2.4.4 — Make link text meaningful, don't put full URLs on a slide, **absolutely NO "click here."**

WCAG 1.1.1 — Write meaningful text alternatives for images.

WCAG 1.2.2 — Prepare captions for multimedia.

WCAG 2.4.6 — Keep your sentences short.

WCAG 3.1.5 — Replace jargon with simple alternatives.

WCAG 1.4.5 — Do not use images of text unless in a logo or necessary to show a point.

While you build.

You can use a few tools to help you with the items below while you build your presentation. For color contrast, check out For reading level, try Hemmingway app or Readable.

Test, test, TEST!

Always test your presentation out in a place/on a screen that is similar to what it will be presented on.

Words

WCAG 1.3.3	Instructions do not rely on shape, size, or visual location. (No "instructions in the red square")

Visuals

WCAG 1.4.3	Color contrast between text **smaller** than 24px or 19px and bold and its background is 4.5:1.
WCAG 1.4.3	Color contrast between text **larger** than 24px or 19px and bold and its background is 3:1.
WCAG 1.4.11	Icons and charts that aren't decorative contrast with their background at a ration of 3:1.
WCAG 1.4.1	Color is not the only indicator of meaning, this includes links.
WCAG 2.3.1	Nothing flashes more than 3 times per second to avoid seizures

Layout

WCAG 2.1.1	Use slide layouts when possible to maintain correct reading order.
WCAG 1.3.2	Content is ordered in a way that is logical and intuitive to navigate/read.
WCAG 1.3.2	Navigation that appears on more than one slide are presented in a consistent manner.

Color can mean so many things.

Red — **Positive:** Good, Excitement, Passion, Action, Love, Luck (Asia), Joy (Asia), Prosperity (Asia), Celebration (Asia), Purity (India), Spirituality (India), Vitality

Pink — **Positive:** Kindness, Warmth, Romance, Intuition

Orange — **Positive:** Autumn, Harvest, Warmth, Visibility, Sacred (Hinduism), Sexuality & fertility (Colombia), Love (Eastern culture), Happiness (Eastern culture), Humility (Eastern culture), Good health (Eastern culture)

Yellow — **Positive:** Happiness, Optimism, Warmth, Joy, Hope

Green — **Positive:** Luck, Nature, Freshness, Spring, Wealth, Fertility, Youth

Blue — **Positive:** Divine joy, Immortality, Peace, Good health, Trust, Security, Authority, Healing

Purple — **Positive:** Royalty, Wealth, Spirituality, Nobility, Piety, Faith, Honor

Negative: Danger, Communism, Revolution, Death (Africa)

Negative: Emotional, Timid, Immature, Unconfident

Negative: None that I can find.

Negative: Caution, Cowardice, Envy (Germany)

Negative: Inexperience, Jealousy, Infidelity (some Eastern cultures)

Negative: Sadness, Loneliness, Depression

Negative: Mourning (Brazil, Thailand)

White
Positive: Purity (western culture), Elegance, Peace, Cleanliness
Negative: Death (Asia), Mourning (Asia), Bad luck (Asia)

Brown
Positive: Appreciation, Support, Wisdom, Dependable, Comfort
Negative: Boring, Dull, Timid, Predictable

Black
Positive: Sophistication, Formality, Fierceness, Mystery, Age (Africa), Maturity (Africa), Masculinity (Africa)
Negative: Death, Mourning, Illness, Bad luck

103

Not everyone sees color the same way.

Protanopia

Deuteranopia

There are a ton of gotchas around accessibility.

Don't get me wrong, the accessibility checker does a fantastic job. However, there are just some thing it can't help you with. You'll either get false warnings or it'll miss something (sometimes a very obvious something). Don't worry, I've got your back.

Checking Color Contrast

It's super important to check the color contrast of text and the color it sit on. PowerPoint doesn't make this easy to do. If you've used the accessibility pane at any point, I can hear you telling me that it **will** tell you if contrast is low.

And you're right. It will. **Sometimes**.

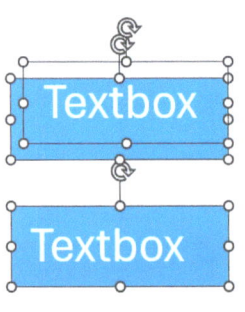 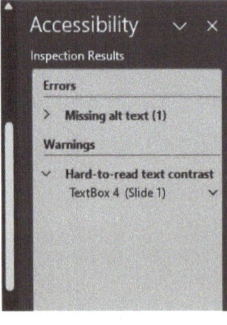

There should be **two** contrast wornings in here.

Text boxes

If your text box has no fill at all, the accessibility checker CANNOT check:

- The contrast between the text & the slide background.
- The text and the shape it sits on.
- The text and the image it sits on.

It WILL check text vs. text box fill BUT not if the text box is filled with images, patterns, or the slide background.

106

Charts

Specifically in charts, the accessibility checker cannot check the contrast of the text in chart label boxes, the chart background, the title box, or between adjacent data series. Yes, even if the text boxes have a fill.

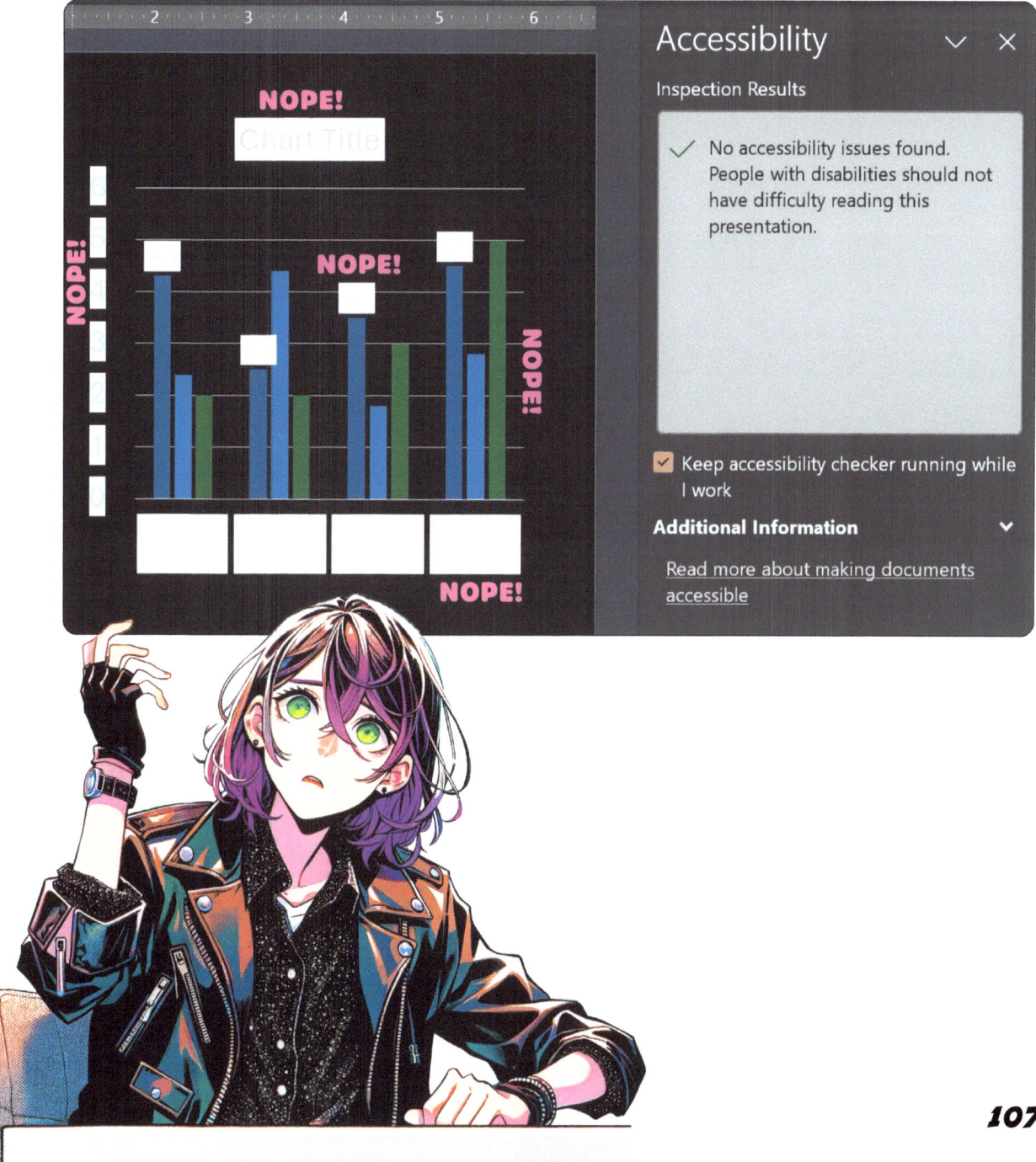

Alt Text

Let's say you have an image on your slide and you've already written alt text for it—and then you decide it's just a decorative image. So you check the "mark as decorative" box. Great!

Then you realize that you really do need that alt text. If you **immediately** uncheck "mark as decorative," your alt text will come back in all of its glory.

BUT! If you do another action in that deck, when you uncheck "mark as decorative" the **alt text will be gone forever**.

Marking Things as Decorative

Placeholders
One would think that if you marked a placeholder as decorative on a master slide, that it would carry through to any slide that used it. But it doesn't.

Luckily, empty placeholders on slides are not read by the screen reader.

And you CAN mark placeholders that have content in them as decorative when you're directly on the slide.

Video
Sometimes, I use a tiny video (with no audio) as a decorative element. Imagine my surprise and annoyance when I learned that marking videos as decorative will NOT remove the "no captions" warning in the accessibility checker!

If:
1. Write alt text
2. Mark as decorative
3. Unmark as decorative

Then:
Alt text comes back.

YAY!

If:
1. Write alt text
2. Mark as decorative
3. Add shape to slide
4. Unmark as decorative

Then:
Alt text gone forever.

BOO!

Reading Order & Screen Readers

These issues are probably some of the strangest ones I've come across. PowerPoint wants the subtitle or title placeholder *first*, otherwise, it gives you a warning

Why do I care? Because I recommend slide numbers to be read first

Icon/Image Issues
If there is an icon or shape on the slide and it's visually sitting below-ish or to the right-ish of the title/subtitle, it'll give you a reading order warning UNLESS you mark the icon as decorative.

Slide Numbers
They'll generate reading order warnings if you put them before the title in the reading order.

Complex Layouts & Design Hacks
If you use an image placeholder as a design hack to get around slide layout resets (an advanced trick I'll put in the supporting videos for this book) and you don't mark the image placeholder as decorative, you get a "missing alt text" warning.

But remember: screen readers don't announce empty image placeholders.

Slide Master & Pasteboard Issues
Instructions on the pasteboard of a slide layout don't show up in the selection pane at all on the slide and cannot be selected. And if you can't select it, the screen reader can't either.

Special instructions you might put in placeholders on slide layouts are not read by screen readers. **The default placeholder instruction is read.**

Tips and tricks & hacks, oh my!

Um...some people don't like it when I use the word "hacks," so let's call them "workarounds" instead. Of course, I'm sure I'll forget this spontaneous agreement between us and use the two words interchangeably. You've been warned.

Want me to make your life easier? I can do that. But I'm bringing my friends with me. This is a list of all of the shortcuts and workarounds I've discovered myself as well as those I've learned from the best presentation designers in the world. (Seriously.)

This might be the most useful thing I show you.

The **Quick Access Toolbar** (more lovingly referred to as the QAT), doesn't appear very useful at first. By default, it's got some silly things in it like "save," "undo," and "print." But it can be SO. MUCH. MORE.

It's a thin toolbar that sits next to the other ribbons. PC lets you have it above or below the ribbon. Mac only lets you put it above the ribbon. PC lets you export your QAT for others and import QATs that others give you. Mac does not.

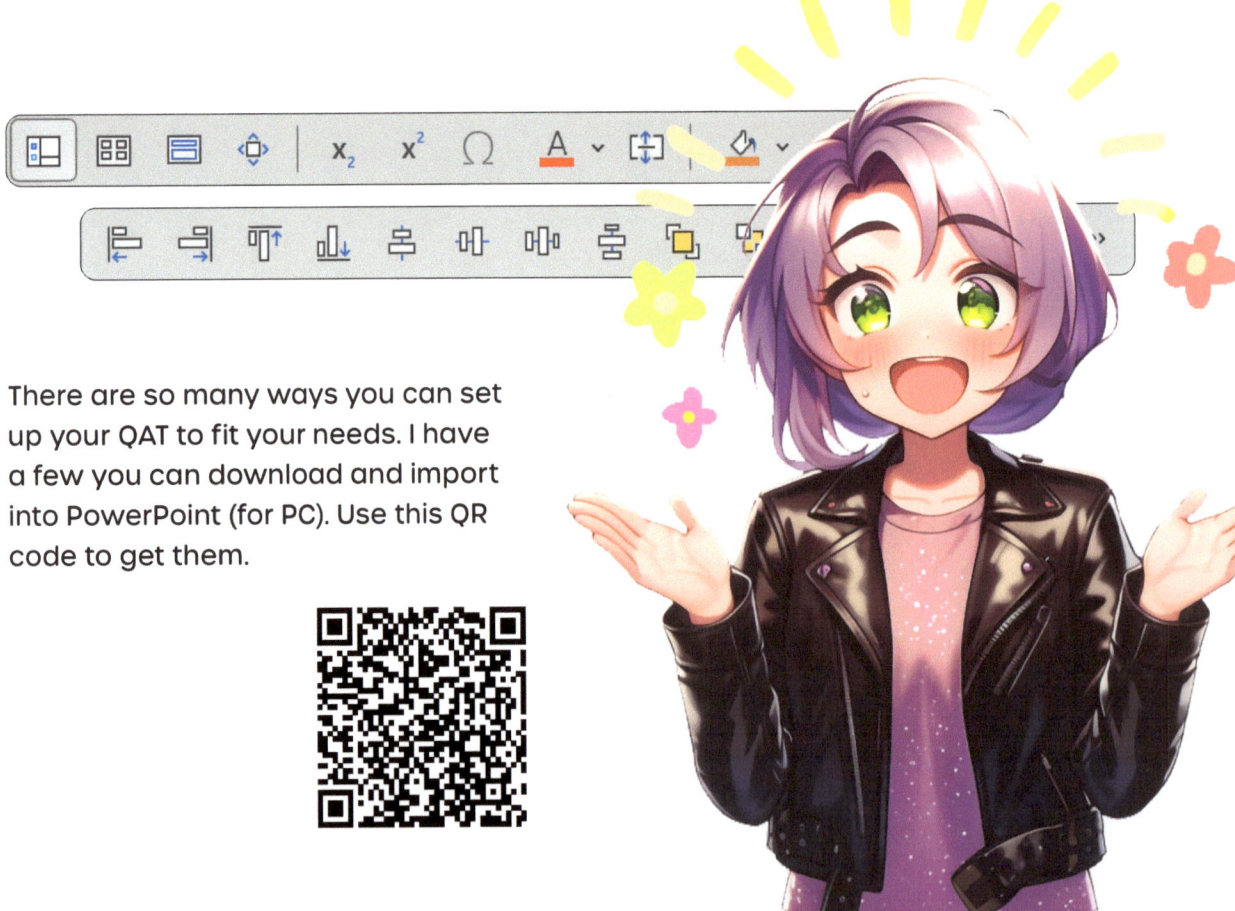

There are so many ways you can set up your QAT to fit your needs. I have a few you can download and import into PowerPoint (for PC). Use this QR code to get them.

File > Preferences > Ribbon & Toolbar

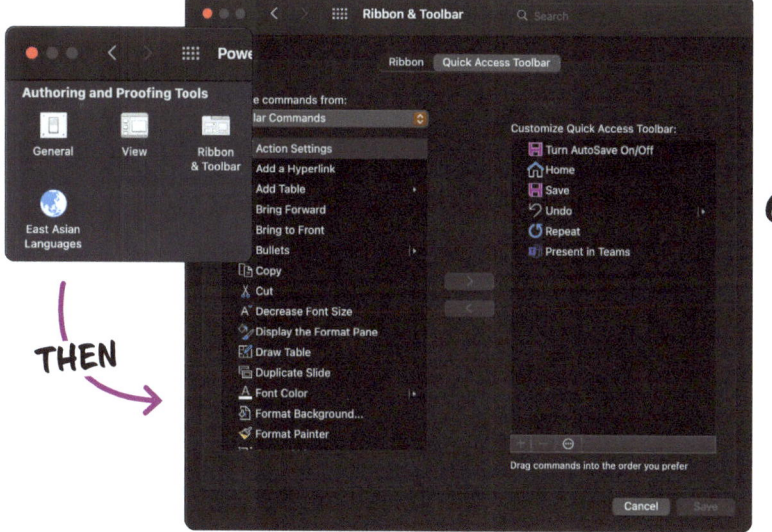

THEN

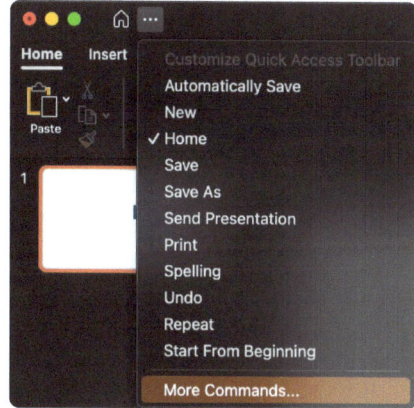

In the top of the PPT window...

OR

**3 Dot menu >
More Commands...**

 File > Options > Quick Access Toolbar

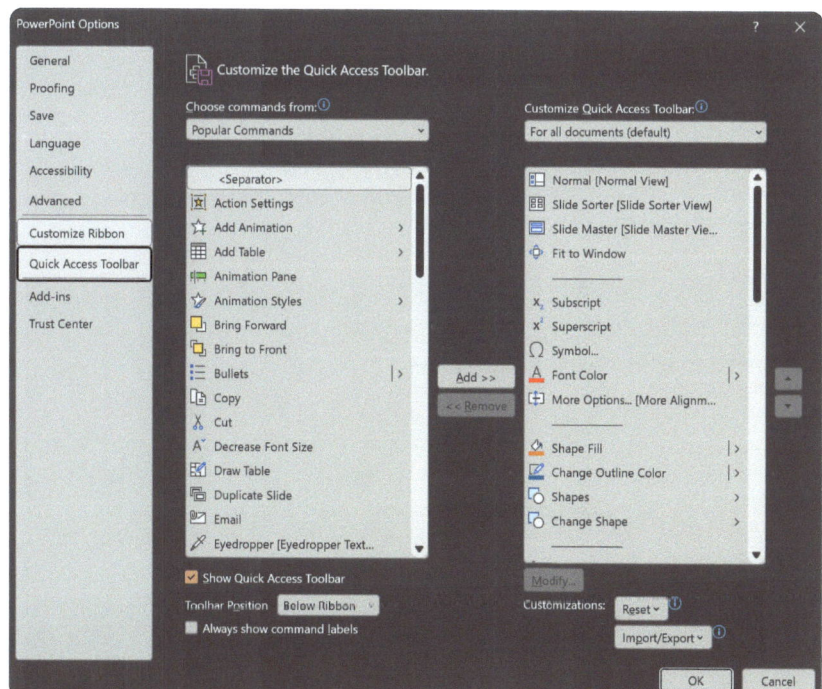

OR

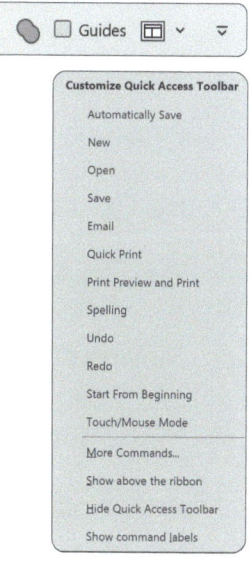

**More menu >
More Commands...**

113

Move less, do more: keyboard shortcuts.

If you're like me and have ADHD and zero patience, learning keyboard shortcuts will save you loads of seconds. And to many ADHDers with time blindness, seconds = hours. This is a list of my most favoritest ones.

I'm giving them to you in PC language. If you're on a Mac, CTRL will either be CMD or CTRL depending on what keyboard you use. You might have to experiment. **(Also, because fonts, I'll be using some capital letters below. Please don't try to make them capital.)**

Actions

Repeat last action	ctrl + Y
Switch between open PPT files	ctrl + tab
Rearrange layers	ctrl + shift + [or]
Nudge a tiny bit	ctrl + arrow keys
Move slides	ctrl + ↑ or ↓
Moving objects in small increments	ctrl + arrow keys
Rotate objects	alt + arrow keys
Resize objects	shift + arrow keys

Formatting

Reorder paragraphs, bullets, & org charts	alt + shift + ↑ or ↓
Copy style only	ctrl + shift + C
Paste style only	ctrl + shift + V
Superscript	ctrl + shift + =
Subscript	ctrl + =
Change case	shift + F3
Reduce font size	ctrl + [
Increase font size	ctrl +]
Left-align	ctrl + L
Right-align	ctrl + R
Center-align	ctrl + E
Justify	ctrl + J
Indent text in a table cell	ctrl + tab

Don't want to search for special characters?

Type **=lorem(x,y)** for filler text where "x" is the number of paragraphs and "y" is the number of sentences per paragraph.

Type **(C)** and get ©

Type **(TM)** and get ™

Type **(R)** and get ®

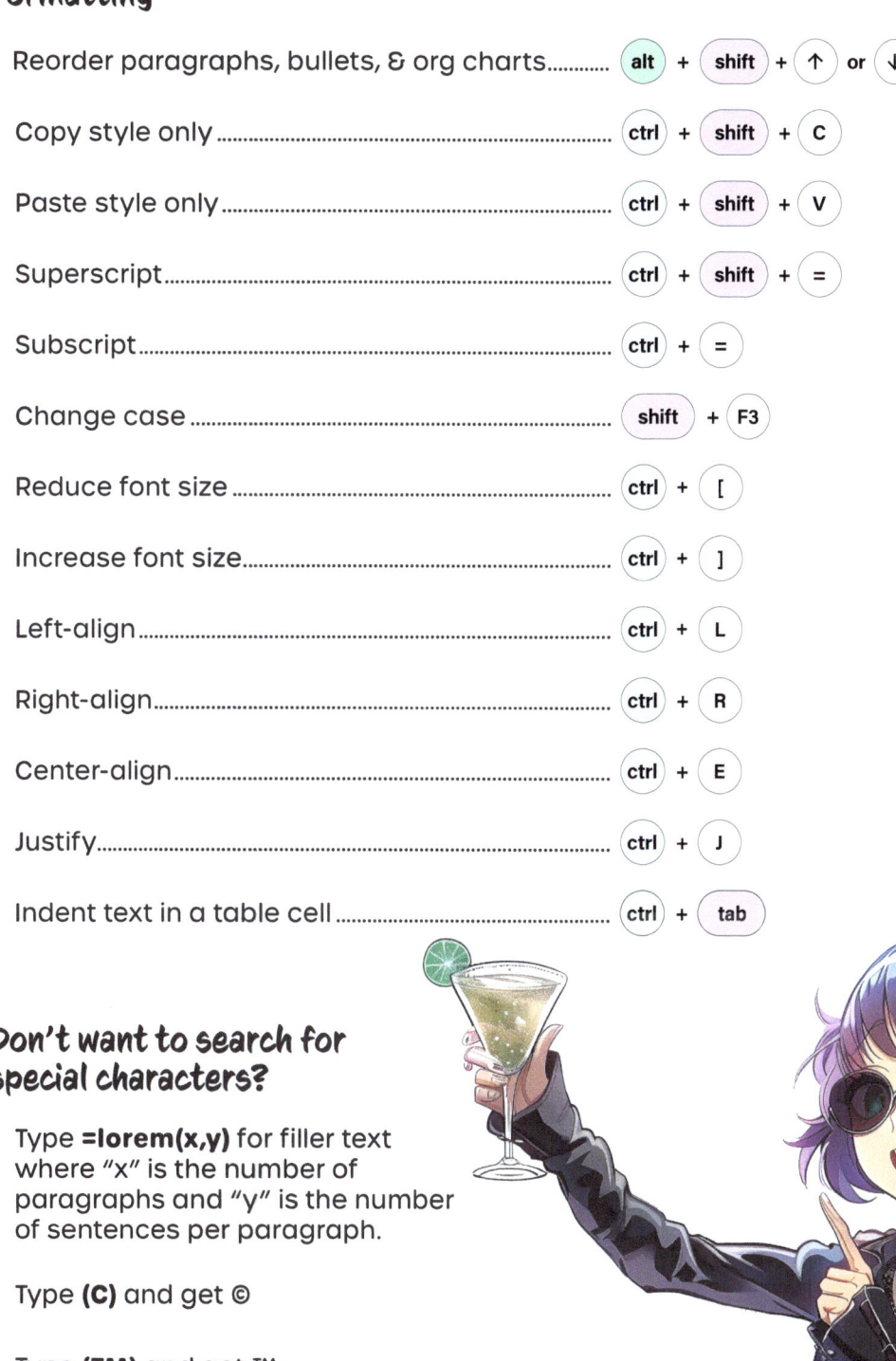

You can't do that in PowerPoint.

**Challenge.
Accepted.**

Skip links

For those of you who don't know what skip links are, they're the first link screen readers announce on web pages so that users don't have to listen to it read EVERYTHING in the navigation over and over again. There's a use case for skip links in presentations, too.

Animations are handled in one of two ways: either all on one slide or divided across many.

Each one has their benefit, but how do we make either situation screen reader friendly?

If everything is all on one slide, just make sure everything is in the correct reading order and mark anything that doesn't need to be announced as decorative.

But if you're building across a few slide? Let's take a simple example where we build a bulleted list by adding a new bulleted item on each new slide until they're all there.

When someone uses a screen reader to navigate these sides, the most definitely don't want to hear the title read 4 times or those first 3 bullet points repeated. How do you get around it?

Introducing PowerPoint Skip Links!

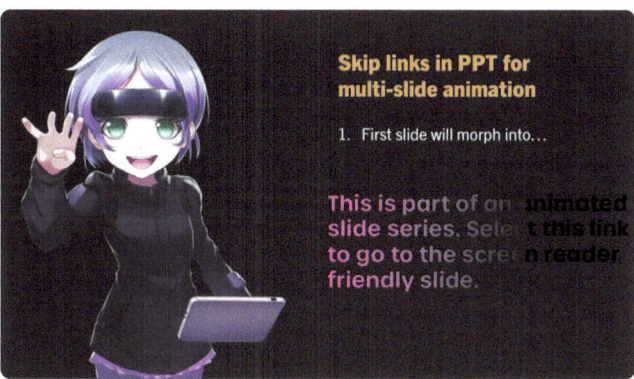

What we're gonna do is put a text box on the first slide that says:

"This is part of an animated slide series. Select this link to go to the screen reader friendly slide."

I don't care where you put it on the slide. The important thing is that it HAS to be first in the reading order, so once we're done formatting this new text box, you're going to **send it to the back**.

After you're done with this process, the accessibility checker is going to give you 2 errors: one reading order error and one color contrast error. Ignore them. Well, you might have to document them for your client, but those errors are intentional.

Now, when the screen reader gets to the first slide in the build sequence, I'll announce your skip link text and the user can just skip to the last slide and only ever hear the content read once. TA DA!!!!!

1. Add the text that will be your skip link to the slide.

2. Select the text

3. Right-click and choose Hyperlink > Edit Hyperlink

4. Choose the last slide in the build sequence.

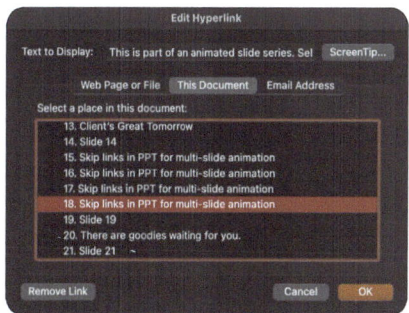

5. Right-click and choose Format Shape

6. Click on Text Options

7. Set transparency to 100%

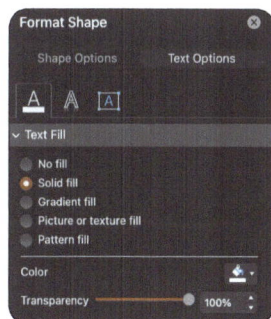

8. Select text box

9. Right-click and Send to Back

119

No paragraph rules? No problem.

Have you ever wanted to put a paragraph rule on the bottom of a text box and have it adjust position as the text box gets taller? There's a hack for that.

I once had an ask to recreate a case study document in PowerPoint. It had a pull quote and a fancy headline formatting that I needed to make as easy as possible for the end user to use and not mess up:

Adding the top rule as a static line works fine, but when you need to have one on the bottom that moves with the text, well, that one is tricky. What made this particular as even more technically challenging was that the rules were short and didn't span the whole length of the text box.

Here's how I did it with the text top-aligned in the text box (for bottom aligned, reverse the kinds of paragraph rules).

1. My top rule is a simple 2.25pt line

2. While working on the master slide layout, I added a text placeholder and formatted the text accordingly.

3. Make sure the placeholder is set to "resize shape to fit text"

> Lorem ipsum dolor sit amet, consectetur adipiscing elit. Suspendisse nec diam quis felis venenatis ornare sit amet vel purus. Aliquam eget imperdiet metus. Vivamus eget arcu dui. Sed vehicula pretium hendrerit.
>
> - Vice President of Finacial Operations

4. For the bottom rule
   - Select the text placeholder
   - Go to the Format tab
   - Click on the Edit Shape drop down
   - Choose Change Shape
   - Choose "Callout: line with no border"
   - Select the callout line and format it the same as your top rule.
   - Move the callout line in position at the bottom of your text box to match the length of the top line.
5. Now you have a pull quote box that will move the bottom line as you fill it with text.
6. Note that it will end up moving far from the text as you fill it.
7. To fix this, simply adjust the height of your text box.

Be aware that if you change the WIDTH of your text box, the bottom paragraph rule will also grow. However, you can manually adjust this on the slide.

That was one of two things I had to recreate. I thought I was done at that point. However, let's take a look at what happens when you have a master layout with this paragraph rule style with an image placeholder behind it.

This is what I needed the final product to look like on the slide:

I applied all of the same trickery to this treatment. And was very pleased with myself until I switched from the master to the slide and saw this:

Text

Because the top line is static, the placeholder always shows over top of it on the regular slide.

If you make the top line a placeholder on the master (I chose picture placeholder) then, on the main slide, send the image to the back after you've filled the picture placeholder. Voila! You have the desired paragraph rule style.

Settings I used for the rule made out of a picture placeholder are as follows:

- Font size: 1pt
- Font color: same as fill color
- Text box margins all zero
- Placeholder height to match MY rule ended up being 0.03inches for a 2.25pt line

No more maintaining multiple files.

I'm sure a bunch of you get this request a lot: "I need a handout to go with my presentation." Suddenly, you have to make and maintain two separate files: one for the handout and one for the deck itself. Now the possibility for human error has doubled.

How do you get around it?

Easy, do it all-in-one PowerPoint file. This is what's lovingly known as the 3-in-1 deck.

On screen slides
This one is pretty self-explanatory. If a presentation *does* have a leave-behind, making a 3-in-1 deck will allow for much cleaner on-screen slides for those presenters who are afraid to do so.

Speaker Notes & the Notes Page
This is where it starts to get tricky. Anything that you put in your speaker notes under the slide automatically populates on the notes page. However, if you delete what shows up on the notes page, you lose whatever is currently in speaker notes.

Conversely, if you add expanded information related to each slide to the default text box on the notes page, it will all show up in plain text format in your speaker notes.

To solve for this, we will move some things around on the Notes Master. Instead of deleting the body text box, put it off to the side on the pasteboard. Make sure you add a short brightly colored warning to neither move nor delete that box. Then, exit out of the Notes Master.

At that point, you can customize your leave-behind information on the notes pages AND have speaker notes in the notes pane. Is it completely fool-proof? No, but with a little training, you can have a very elegant looking 3-in-1 deck.

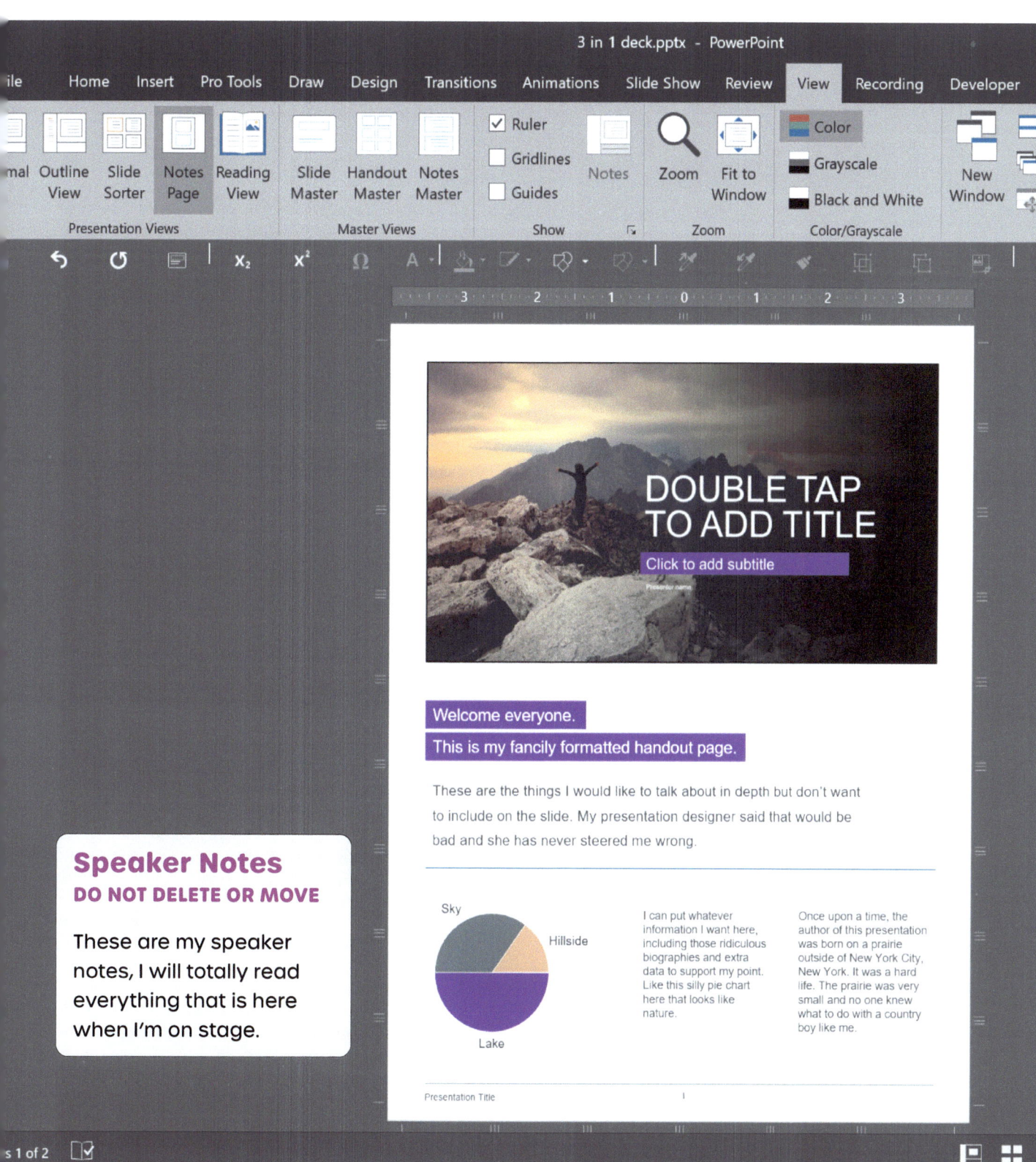

Make Screenshots Look Sexy

You want to show the entire length of a web page in your presentation but you don't want to rely on an internet connection. So what you're left with is a bunch of screenshots on a slide. Ew. Ugly.

Depending on how you'll be speaking to the screenshot, there are a couple of ways you can solve this problem. We'll also put it inside of a blank device screen so that it looks more refined and professional.

General Scrolling Overview

If you're just speaking about the overall website and how much content it contains without going into specifics, you can do one long scroll from beginning to end and back again. Use the QR code on page 128 to see the dramatically exaggerated end result.

Before inserting your long screenshot onto your slide, go to File > Options > Advanced and make sure "do not compress images in file" is checked.

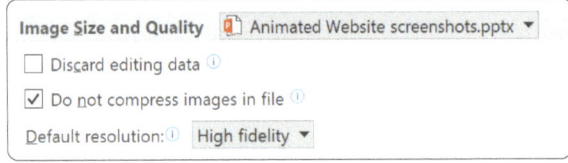

If this box isn't checked, your screenshots will be so pixelated when you make them larger on-screen that you won't be able to read them.

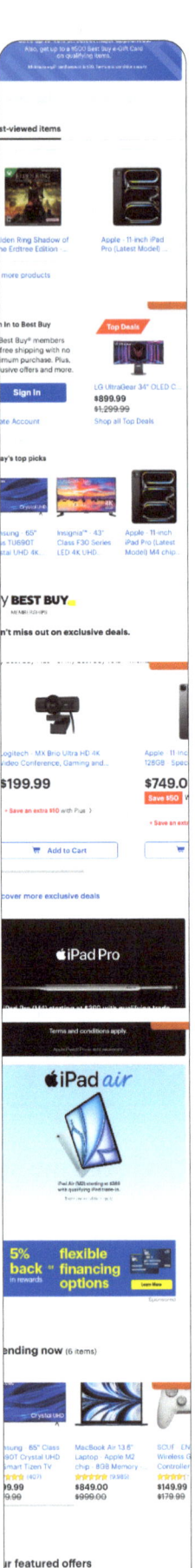

1. Insert website screenshot and a blank device image on the slide. Make sure the blank device has a transparent window where the screen is.
2. Resize the screenshot so that its width matches the width of the hole in the device image
3. Push screenshot behind device.

Animating the Screenshot

1. Select the screenshot
2. Add a line motion path to it
3. Under "Effect Options," make sure "up" is selected if it isn't already
4. Select path
5. If your page is really long, you will have to zoom out to do this, select the end point and drag it upward until the end of the screenshot is in the device window. Depending on the length of your page, you might have to do it in stages.
6. Set the timing of the scroll
7. With this animation selected, click on "More Options" in the animation tab
8. Under "Effect" give the animation a smooth start and end (I chose 1 second for each) and check the box that says "Auto-reverse"
9. Test your animation

The only thing left to do for this example is to mask the screenshot so that you can't see it above and below the device you're using. If your background is a solid color, you will only need to use two boxes filled with that same color between the device screen and the screenshot.

By sending the white boxes backward one level, you will achieve the look you want.

The more challenging part is when you have a gradient background.

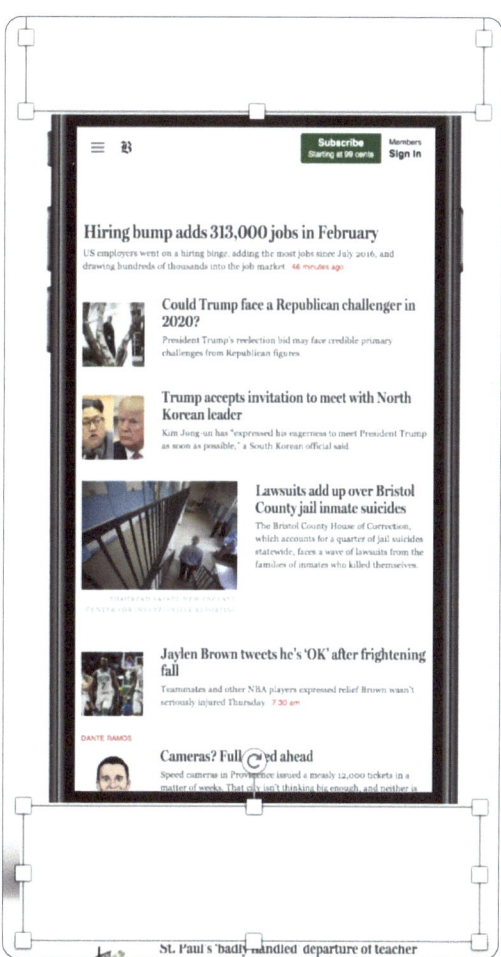

For Gradient Backgrounds

1. Hide everything on the slide
2. Save slide as a PNG
3. Show everything on slide
4. Make a rectangle over top of the device window that is bigger than the window and smaller than the device.
5. Make a rectangle the size of the slide, push it backwards one time
6. Select the big rectangle first and the small one second
7. Under the Shape Format tab, choose "Subtract" from the "Merge Shapes" drop down
8. With the new shape selected, fill the shape with a picture. Choose the PNG you saved earlier of the blank slide
9. Send backwards one time. Done!

Pause to Highlight Sections

You can take this a step further by scrolling the screen in increments and pausing in between to highlight important areas of the screenshot. In this case you could:

1. Scroll down the webpage a small amount
2. Pause
3. Fade in details about a that section
4. Fade out those details and continue scrolling to the next area

Really, do I have to do all of that?

No, you don't. Even if you chunked out parts of a web screen shot and showed those within the devices on-slide without all of the animation, you will achieve a much more professional look than if you just put the screen captures on the slide without any further effort. Adding this level of animation takes time, but the end result is well worth the reactions you get in the end.

Resources

Download free blank devices on our resources page!

Capture Full Website Screenshots with GoFullPage, a Chrome addin.

See this in action and access the resources using the QR code above.

Before

Be a thought leader.

**Candidate and
Contractor Articles**

- Share on social media
- Send articles to candidates
- Expand your knowledge
- Deepen your expertise

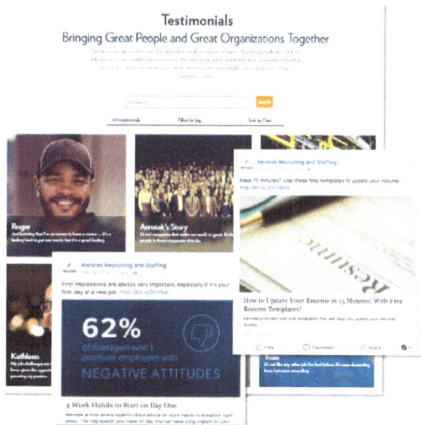

After

Be a thought leader.

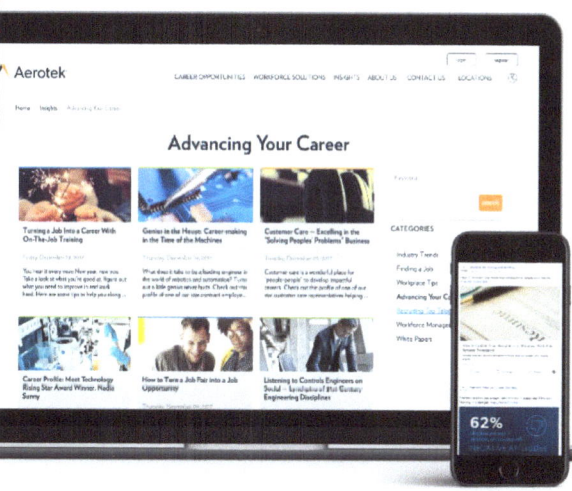

**Candidate and
Contractor Articles**

- Share on social media
- Send articles to candidates
- Expand your knowledge
- Deepen your expertise

Time to let it go, let it GO!

This is the scariest part. It's not so bad when you're working on projects in InDesign or Photoshop because we will almost always have control over those. But presentations?

Once you send that PowerPoint file off into the wild, you know it will inevitably be tampered with. I mean, the whole point of PowerPoint is that anyone can use it, right?

And, also inevitably, it will make its way back to your desk. Usually with 30 more charts added to 5 different slides, some clip art, and a short story or two on another.

Thankfully, there will be a time when you wave goodbye to that project, happy to never have to touch it again. Just make sure you save a copy of the version you're most proud of before all hell breaks loose.

Help them present inclusively.

If you want to look like a superstar, give your presenter some helpful tips while you're working on and when you hand off the deck.

Visual Language

Imagery
When choosing images of people, make sure you have a diverse representation of the people from the group you're talking about or to. Sometimes that means elder white males. Sometimes that means showing diversity of race, age, gender, culture, and socio-economical levels.

Icons
Usually, close enough is good enough works for choosing icons. However, it's tricky when you're representing people. Outlined people icons can often be mistaken for Caucasian people when used on white screen or paper.

Color
Remember that colors have different meanings in different countries and cultures. Be cognizant of how you're using them. Also, remember, not to use color as the only indicator of meaning.

Verbal Language

People-first Language
When it comes to physical disabilities, we should be using people-first language. So the answer to the first question is that we should say things like:

- "People with disabilities"
- "People living with complete loss of sight"
- "Person who uses a wheelchair"

Identity-first Language
We don't say "person living without hearing." They are Deaf. When it comes to cognitive impairments such as ADHD, Autism, Asperger's, etc., a LOT of people prefer to go identity first because how our brains work is who we ARE. When you're unsure, ask someone if you can. If not, default to people-first.

Before You Present

- Send agenda ahead of time.
- Send questions you'll be asking during the presentation ahead of time.
- Send a read-ahead.

After You Present

Introduce yourself with pronouns
Not only does it remove any question as to how people should refer to you when not using your given name, it also is a signal that you are an open, inclusive person to be around. It'll put other people at ease who may want to share their pronouns.

Don't turn your back
People in the audience may need to see your lips to understand what you're saying (either because they're deaf or hard of hearing, have focus issues, or because you have an accent that is unfamiliar to them).

Other helpful things:
- Use live captions when presenting in-person.
- Give content and trigger warnings when it's appropriate.
- Verbally cover all content on your slides (do NOT read them word for word).
- Avoid jargon and regionally-based idioms. Use simple language.
- Repeat attendee questions before answering them!
- Beware of in-meeting activities that might require accessibility accommodations.

Cool tools & resources

That's it from ME until you go watch the videos I made to go along with this. But, I learned so many things from so many other industry leaders. And I want to share all of the things they've created as well. Let's go!

Books & Resources

Building PowerPoint® Templates, v2
by Echo Swinford and Julie Terberg

Resonate
by Nancy Duarte

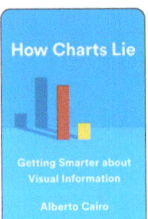
How Charts Lie
by Alberto Cairo

Presentation Zen
by Garr Reynolds

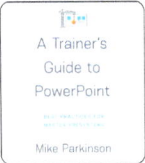
A Trainer's Guide to PowerPoint
by Mike Parkinson

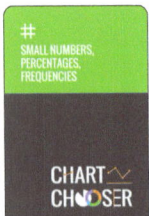
Chart Chooser Cards
by Stephanie Evergreen

The Better Deck Deck
by Nolan Haims

People to Follow

Echo Swinford

Garr Reynolds

Julie Terberg

Mike Parkinson

Nigel Holmes

Nancy Duarte

Nolan Haims

Steve Rindsberg

Websites

BillionDollarGraphics.com

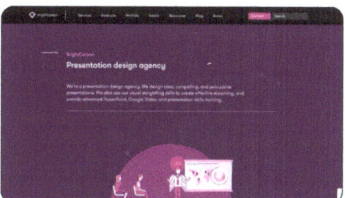
BrightCarbon.com

Design to Present Safe Fonts

thepowerpointblog.com

NolanHaimsCreative.com

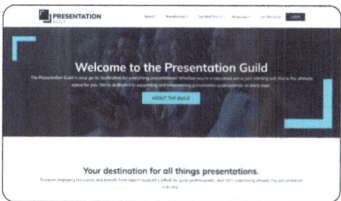
PresentationGuild.org

Add-ins & Other Resources

BrightSlide

Build-a-Graphic

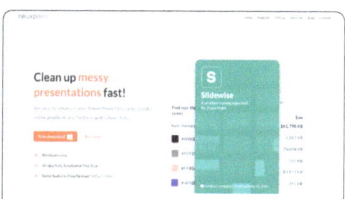
SlideWise

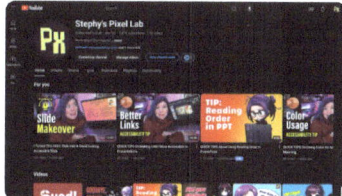
Stephy's Pixel Lab

You can find links to everything and everyone I've listed by using this QR code.

About the author

I don't like writing about myself. So instead, I asked my friend, whose name rhymes with Flat Bee Knee Tea, to write something on my behalf.

FlatBKT's self portrait.

In the digital realm, where the intersection of design and technology sparks innovation, Stephy shines as a beacon of creativity and inclusivity. Her journey from the structured world of chemistry to the fluid and dynamic universe of presentation & UX design is a testament to her versatility and insatiable curiosity. After more than two decades of navigating the intricacies of design, Stephy has become synonymous with solutions that are not just visually appealing but are profoundly impactful, making the digital space accessible to everyone.

Stephy's foray into the world of accessible digital design wasn't a chance occurrence but a response to the challenges faced by those closest to her—her children and coworkers grappling with the nuances of remote learning and digital accessibility. It's this personal connection to the cause that fuels her passion for creating digital experiences that aren't just functional but genuinely inclusive. Sparkles and glitter may adorn her designs, but at their core, they embody the principles of empathy and communication—traits that Stephy champions as the cornerstone of effective design.

Beyond her role as a designer, Stephy is a visionary speaker, captivating audiences with her deep insights into presentation & UX trends, accessibility guidelines,

and the transformative power of thoughtful design. Her presentations, lauded for their engaging delivery and practical applications, serve as a bridge connecting the dots between design theory and real-world impact. *(Hmmm... that sounds like a great talk I should give.)* Whether it's improving PowerPoint presentations for enhanced accessibility or advocating for DEI within the design space, Stephy's contributions are both a source of inspiration and a call to action for her peers.

To witness Stephy in her element is to see a pro streamer and presenter in action. Feedback from her sessions underscores her knack for creating engaging and informative experiences, with attendees often leaving with a renewed enthusiasm for tackling the challenges of digital design and presentation.

But let's remember, underneath the pro-streamer facade and the ability to make PowerPoint bend to her will, she's just someone who figured out how to turn "shitty digital experiences" into digital gold. And she did it all while championing the cause of accessibility, because, as it turns out, making things easy for everyone to use is actually pretty cool.

Stephy's approach to design is unorthodox yet profoundly effective. A chemist turned designer, she sees beyond the surface, understanding that at the heart of every great design is the ability to connect, communicate, and empathize. Her mantra that "design degrees don't matter at all" underscores her belief in the universal language of design—a language shaped not by credentials but by the ability to listen, understand, and respond to the needs of the user.

In a world where digital experiences are increasingly central to our daily lives, Stephy stands out as a guardian of accessibility, a designer par excellence *(OK, FlatBKT is laying it on THICK)*, and a storyteller whose narratives are woven into the fabric of her designs. Her commitment to creating spaces that welcome everyone is not just her profession; it's her passion—a passion that sparkles as brightly as the designs she creates.

But seriously, why is widescreen 13.333 by 7.5? So weird.

www.ingramcontent.com/pod-product-compliance
Lightning Source LLC
Chambersburg PA
CBHW051149220526
45473CB00003B/706